MIDI Survival Guide

MIDI Survival Guide

Vic Lennard

PC Publishing

PC Publishing
4 Brook Street
Tonbridge
Kent TN9 2PJ
UK

First published 1993

© PC Publishing

ISBN 1 870775 28 7

British Library Cataloguing in Publication Data

Lennard, Vic
 MIDI Survival Guide
 I. Title
 780.285

ISBN 1-870775-28-7

Phototypesetting by Hilary Norman Design
Printed and bound in Great Britain by BPCC Wheatons, Exeter

Foreword

Dan Goldstein
Editor, *Home & Studio Recording*

When MIDI first appeared a decade ago, it was dismissed by studio professionals as being too simple to be of much use. Today, after ten years in which MIDI has changed the lives of thousands of people working in music and recording, it is the system's complexity, rather than its simplicity, that is the stumbling block for many.

It seems that with each step along the path of sophistication, MIDI succeeds in adding another series of techno-headaches. And, now that MIDI has permeated almost every stage of composing, arranging, recording and even performing music, the scope for confusion and bewilderment is greater than ever.

This is the main reason why I'm so delighted Vic Lennard, our Technical Consultant on *Home & Studio Recording*, has found time to write this book. There have been MIDI reference works before. But, without exception, they have been one of three things: obsessed with digital theory; littered with irrelevant references to specific hardware and software; or downright condescending.

You know what you want MIDI to do for your music - you don't need to know its hexadecimal equivalent. You like what your technology can do - you don't want to be told to go out and buy something else. And, above all, you want to learn without being lectured.

If any of the above sentiments sounds familiar, this book is for you. In fact, I'd go as far as to say it's for anyone who's serious enough about their music to want to get the best from MIDI. Because, at its best, MIDI can be one of the most musically creative innovations of the last ten years.

So what are you waiting for? Plug in and go!

Acknowledgments

My gratitude to Helen for providing the atmosphere and food at *Helensholme*, the perfect place for me to write this book.

Thanks to my parents, daughter Tamar, and especially my wife, Sharon, for their constant support over the years. Also to Paul Simmons, my long-term music partner, for ideas and proof reading.

Finally, a special thanks to my son, Sam, who has helped to keep me sane and given me a better perspective on life.

Contents

Introduction

Everyone has entered their local hi-tech music shop and stared longingly at the never-ending rows of equipment. Synths, sound modules, effects units, mixing desks, multi-track tape recorders ... the list is almost endless. Even worse is the fact that many new units are added each month. This only makes the question of 'what shall I buy for my MIDI system' that little bit more difficult to answer.

For those of you looking to buy your first piece of MIDI equipment, welcome to the MIDI-go-round! If you are already on-board and reading this, you are either interested in upgrading parts of your MIDI system or filling the gaps that exist. Of course, you may have already completed your equipment purchases and now need to know how to piece your system together. How do I connect my sequencer to my synth? My drum machine doesn't have a MIDI Thru - what can I do? How do I get my sequencer to run in time with my 4-track recorder? These questions, and many more, will be answered in this book.

If you are a typical MIDI user who wants to create music but cannot get your teeth around the nitty-gritty of putting together a MIDI system, this book will prove to be invaluable to you. It will take you from the initial considerations you should be making through to having a smoothly working MIDI system. In short, this book will show you how to survive with MIDI.

Planning your system

What is a MIDI system?

A MIDI system is a collective term for all the equipment you need to be able to record music. This includes a sequencer, which may be a computer running a sequencing program or a dedicated unit, synths and sound modules, effects processors and any of the small black boxes that are necessary to ensure the smooth running of such a set-up. If it is your intention to record to tape then a multi-track tape recorder and a sync unit should also be included under the same heading. Why? Because the music you record on tape must be in time with any MIDI instruments playing via the sequencer. This aspect is usually called synchronisation and will be covered fully in Chapter 7. Suffice to say that a multi-track recorder should really be viewed as part and parcel of a MIDI system.

With such a large number of different items, it is easy to see why many people find it awkward to decide exactly what to buy. Having made a decision, the next problem is finding out where to position the various pieces of equipment and how to cable them together. At this point, you invariably find out that you are short of MIDI leads, audio leads, mains sockets and the like - all the little things that you take for granted.

The mistake most people make is to view their initial MIDI set-up as a complete entity with that rather satisfying feeling of standing back and looking on with pride once the system has been pieced together. Such a feeling invariably lasts for a few days or a couple of weeks at most because once you start to work in anger, so to speak, you always find aspects that start to annoy you. Even though these aspects do not actually get worse with time, they appear to! Consequently, it is important always to allow for a degree of expansion. I doubt whether you will be buying equipment one week and selling it the next - if so, it is unlikely that you would be reading this book - but keeping an open mind is essential if you intend to be truly creative with your MIDI system.

Needs v desire

A trip to a music show or a hi-tech music store with lots of equipment on demonstration can be quite an eye-opener for any musician. It does not matter whether you are a beginner who has yet to make that important first purchase or a seasoned MIDI-user who still has gaps to fill in his system. There is little doubt that some pieces of equipment will appeal more than others. For instance, if you are primarily a keyboard player your interest may be focussed on the latest synth but that should not prevent you from appreciating the other essential items that you will need.

It has probably been said before in various articles, but I'll repeat it here - a shopping list is indispensable. A less popular theory is the idea of two lists. The first has the essential needs for your system while the second is a 'wish list' where all the items that you desire, but may not have budget for, are placed.

Your list of 'needs' might include:
- Velocity-sensitive synth with good on-board sounds, including drums and sound effects.
- Dedicated sequencer with disk drive.
- Multi-timbral sound module with good piano and strings.
- Multi-effects unit with good vocal reverb and guitar chorus.
- Four track recorder with integrated mixer.
  The 'desires' list could contain:
- Pressure-sensitive Master keyboard with weighted keys, preferably 88 notes.
- Computer system with notation program.
- Individual expanders for orchestral and analogue sounds.
- Sampler for looping recorded segments.
- Separate reverb, delay and chorus effects units.
- Eight track recorder with separate mixing desk.

By setting your budget (Chapter 2) and playing off one list against the other, you will probably end up with a couple of items from your second list and most of the first list. Of course, only you can decide the order of importance of items.

You may have noted the constant reference to a MIDI system and not a MIDI studio. This is because the decisions involved are the same whether you are setting up a home recording studio for yourself and, perhaps, a few friends, a small commercial set-up, a major studio or a live performance system.

Live MIDI system

In putting together a live performance system, you will first need a keyboard with MIDI capability. This will either be a synthesiser with its own internal sounds, or a master keyboard which then requires the purchase of one sound module or more. While a master keyboard lacks sounds of its own, it will usually have a superior MIDI design and offer more functions. For example, many master keyboards offer a keyboard split option. This means that all notes above a particular key transmit MIDI information on one MIDI channel while those below that key transmit on a different channel. This allows you to play two different sound from the same keyboard - the left hand might be playing an upright bass while the right plays strings, for example. Some master keyboards offer multiple keyboard splits which then allow you to access more than two sounds in a similar fashion.

Do you need functions such as this for live performance work? Possibly not, but that is a decision you need to make. Buying a master keyboard along with a sound module or two will usually be more expensive than purchasing a synth with its own on-board sounds. Your decision may be tempered by whether you are going to be using your live equipment in a home set-up as well.

Apart from the keyboard and synth side, what else do you need? That depends on how you work live. Many live musicians now use a sequencer which is either a program on a computer or a small dedicated unit. The latter is probably more popular for live work in that it is more robust and is designed for the rigours of being moved around. Many of these will also play MIDI files, a standard method for saving songs on a sequencer so that they can be loaded into other programs, even on other computers.

Typical MIDI system diagrams will be shown in Chapter 3. Other items for live work include an amplifier, mixer with as many inputs as you require, speakers and audio/mains cables.

In the studio

A studio MIDI system is likely to be more comprehensive than a live one because it is essentially a recording environment. It is here that the decision of a master keyboard or a synth with reasonable MIDI capability, including pitch bend and modulation wheels, is a more difficult one to make. If you are intending to build a small home studio setup, the chances are that you will go the route of buying a synth with sounds on-board followed by one or more sound modules. This is fine, and will certainly not be a drawback to working, and recording, with MIDI. Make sure that the synth you buy supports a MIDI feature called Local Control without which you will have problems when using the synth with a sequencer. Such use would not be be impossible, simply more difficult.

Master keyboard or synth, you are still likely to add some sound modules. Look carefully at certain aspects of these:

- Is it multi-timbral - can it play more than one sound simultaneously on many MIDI channels? Such a sound module will give you the capability of almost an orchestra from a single black box.
- How many notes can it play at the same time? This is usually called the polyphony with typical figures being 16 or 24. Just think about what you could do with a synth capable of playing 24 notes simultaneously. If you had a string background sound, a drum kit, bass, brass and, say, lead piano that would only add up to about 15 notes!
- Are certain optional sound cards essential? Are they expensive?
- Does it just contain presets or can you edit the sounds? Can the edited versions be saved?
- In the case of a synth, does it have a Local Control Off facility? If not, its use with a sequencer will be limited (see Chapter 4).

Voices v notes

Be careful how the polyphony is expressed. Some manufacturers do not state a number of notes, but a number of voices, and there is a very real difference because more than one voice may be required to create one sound. For example, a brass sound may be created from two tones, one being trumpet and the other trombone. Each time you press a note on the keyboard, both tones sound. The result is that the polyphony in terms of voices is halved to give the polyphony in terms of notes. The worst point about such a system, which many manufacturers use, is that the actual 'note' polyphony is variable and the only way you know that the polyphony has been exceeded is when you hear sounds cutting out. This is a process called voice-stealing and while it can happen with any synth, it will happen more easily with those that have a lower polyphony.

Which sequencer?

The decision on which sequencer to buy is possibly the most important one. All the main computers offer decent sequencing packages, so the choice of computer is unlikely to be solely down to the musical usage. Thinking along the lines of 'What other use do I want from my computer', answers to certain questions will give you a better indication of which machine to look for:

- Do you want to use it for business - database, spreadsheet and so on?
- Do you need it for graphics and Desktop Publishing?
- Do you want to play games?

As all computers offer acceptable word processors, you are safe in choosing the one with the most suitable sequencer if the only other use is to write a few letters.

If your computer is going to be used purely for music, then you have to look for the package that most fits your needs. To do this, you need to cut down the choice. This can be achieved by going through a list of basic questions:

- Do you want to be able to work with and edit a score? If you do, this will automatically remove half of the possible sequencing programs along with any dedicated units. While budget sequencers with a score edit option can be found, the score editor is invariably limited.

- Do you need to print out notation, and in which case to what level of perfection? Some sequencers allow you to print the basic scores without letting you make many changes to the lay-out. This is fine for, say, printing out a part for a musician but not for publishing your music. A decision on your needs for notation will narrow the field considerably.

- How do you want to work with the sequencer? Have you used a drum machine before? Did you like that manner of working? Many sequencers emulate a drum machine by allowing you to work with patterns that are then arranged together to create a song. If you like this way of working, then look for a pattern-based sequencer - you can normally tell such a beast by the main screen where you can name and move through patterns portraying parts of your song. If you want to create songs in a similar way to that of a multi-track tape recorder, look for a lin-ear-based sequencer that allows you to create songs track by track, instrument by instrument.

One final point. Check if there is an upgrade policy for the sequencer you are considering. Your decision may be influenced by learning that the manufacturer is going to charge you a substantial sum every six or nine months for future upgrades.

Drum machines

For live or studio use, you may wish to consider a drum machine. How do you decide which of the many available models to go for?

- How many sounds does it have on-board? What is their quality and how varied are they? There is little point in your drum sound module having only 30 or so sounds when you intend to use different bass and snare drums for each song. Similarly, if there are 300 sounds but only a handful of snares and bass drums, you are likely to look elsewhere. Following on from this...

- Does it have a card slot for extra sounds? What selection of cards is available and how much do they cost!

- Are the pads big enough and of sufficient sensitivity to be playable? If you are going to use the drum machine as a master, either to record internally or onto an external sequencer, the size and feel of the pads is very important.
- Is there a MIDI In? If not, you cannot use the drum machine as a sound module.
- How big a memory is there for patterns and songs? If you intend to use the drum machine for live work, you are likely to want to have the entire set of songs programmed and in memory. If a drum machine can only hold, say, three songs, it will be useless for your needs.
- Can the memory be dumped to a card, tape or via MIDI? If you are using the drum machine's memory for patterns and songs, you will need to save them externally once the memory is full. If there is a card facility for this, fine, but check the cost of cards. Saving to tape is generally slow and unreliable. If you are also using a sequencer and the drum machine can transfer its memory via MIDI, you have a reliable, and cost-free, means of saving your programming.
- How easily can patterns be edited? The best kind of editing is provided by having a display with a drum grid showing all instruments and the notes that each is playing.
- Does the drum machine have any real time characteristics? For instance, some drum machines give you random fluctuations regarding timing, pitch and loudness which can make drum patterns sound more human in nature.

Samplers

Similarly, many of you will buy a sampler to use custom sounds in your music. How do you decide which one to buy?

- How good is the quality of sound? Look at two of the specifications - the number of bits and the sampling frequency (or rate). Generally, the higher each of these is, the better the sound quality. However, the higher the sampling rate, the more memory used in recording samples, so ...
- What is the initial memory (RAM)? The more memory, the higher the number of seconds of recording that you get, and ...

- Can the memory be expanded? You may find that you use the sampler more and more as time goes by. If the memory can be expanded, the sampler can grow with you.
- Is it multi-timbral? Can you have different sounds assigned to different areas (or zones) of a keyboard, each with its own MIDI channel? If not, you are effectively limited to one sound at a time.
- How many outputs are there? Are they monophonic (one note at a time) or polyphonic (many notes at the same time)? If you only have a stereo pair of outputs, you can't use different effects or different EQ on each of the different sounds that you have selected.
- Is there a decent selection of sounds from either the manufacturer or a third-party library? If you intend to record all your own samples, you won't worry about this. If, however, you want good quality natural instruments like strings, brass or the like, check this out.
- How easily can sounds be looped? Looping is a technique that allows you to take a short recording and make it appear to last forever, essential if you intend to make the most of your sampler's memory. An automatic looping facility is worth its weight in gold.

A few smaller points ...

- Is there a socket for a hard drive (SCSI)? Lots of samples means lots of disks lying around. A hard drive lets you keep the equivalent of many disks in one unit.
- Are there digital inputs and outputs? If you intend to record samples from special sampling CDs, or save your samples to a DAT recorder, such sockets can be very useful.
- Does the sampler support the MIDI standard for transferring samples (MIDI Sample Dump Standard)? If it does, you may be able to transfer sounds from your sampler to your synth.

The main issue ...

- How much does it cost? No matter how good the facilities are, can you afford it ...

Budgeting and buying

Allowing for expansion

The most common mistake made by people setting up a MIDI system is to underestimate the extent by which the system can expand. The most obvious addition is a further sound module or two, especially as the emergence of the latest unit will invariably prompt the appearance of previous models in the second-hand column of various magazines!

Look at what happens to the setting up of your system when you add a sound module. The first problem is where to plug it into the mains; have you allowed enough sockets in your plugboards for further devices, all of which are likely to require mains powering? The second problem depends on how many audio outputs the new sound module has; do you have space for these on your mixer? Chances are that the answer to this will be 'no' in which case you may end up using the stereo outputs from the sound module instead of each of the individual outputs. This compromises the ability to use any effects units on the various instruments playing because they are already mixed together in the stereo outputs. Thirdly, is it possible to connect this new synth into the MIDI side of your system? You may find that you are short of the necessary MIDI Thru from another MIDI device which is likely to be the case if you have two devices without a MIDI Thru. Finally, have you left enough space in the way that you have laid out your studio or live set-up to allow for extra equipment? Don't make the mistake of thinking that you won't buy anything else - you will!

There are ways around these obstacles. For the moment, the first problem can be ignored because the addition of a few extra mains blocks will not affect your financial situation to any great extent. The situation with the required number of mixer inputs is rather different and should really be addressed before the purchase of a mixer (Figure 2-1). You have probably decided on which synths and sound modules to buy; how many outputs do they have? What about the effects unit, or units, that you have decided on; how many outputs do they have? Add together the total number of outputs and to allow for expansion, double

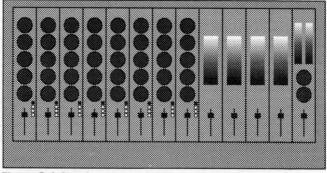

Figure 2-1 Are there enough inputs on your mixer for expansion?

them! The mixer you need to buy may cost you more at the start, but having to buy sub-mixers at a later date or making a loss when reselling the original mixer is likely to be more expensive. Where the MIDI connections are concerned, the next chapter will look at how a MIDI Thru Box can get around the problem of insufficient MIDI Thrus. As for space, make sure that you allow for expansion by leaving a few gaps in a rack unit or part of a surface free.

Basic budgeting rules

Having constructed two lists, one of essential needs and the other of items you would like given no financial restraint, the next move is to work out how much you can afford. The budget you place on yourself must be a realistic one. For instance, there is little point in taking a loan from a bank or otherwise if the monthly repayments cannot be readily met, and that includes the scenario of having to guarantee many hours of commercial work for the studio per day to pay for the investment. The history of the music industry is littered with the remains of such ventures.

- Am I going to buy any of the equipment second-hand? Bargains can certainly be had courtesy of music magazines and used goods in shops, the latter of which will carry some sort of warranty.
- Do I need a special work surface? Allowing for the weight and size of equipment, this is usually a good idea, even if it is only an old metal office desk. Alternatively, consider buying a construction kit made up of bars and connectors that you can cut and build to your custom requirements.
- Will I need keyboard stands? Again, allow for expansion by buying either an 'A' stand that can take more than one keyboard or a stand that can be expanded.
- Do I need a special table for my computer? If you are intending to use a computer, remember that the computer keyboard and monitor need to be in a certain position relative to each other. A computer 'workstation' is worth considering.
- Is much of my intended equipment rackmounted? If so, allow for buying a rack. If the equipment is going to be used live, allow for the extra expense of a flight-cased one.
- Do I want to print music? Do I need to print letters, cassette inlays, address labels and so on? While a 9-pin dot matrix printer is OK for text, allow for at least a 24-pin dot matrix printer or preferably an ink jet or bubble jet variety for the printing out of music notation.
- How good a microphone do I need? Not a MIDI question, but an important one. If you are setting up a commercial studio, you are likely to need a selection.
- Am I going to use a multi-track recorder and a sequencer? If so, you are going to need a sync unit; more about this in Chapter 7.
- Will I use my existing audio system? There is little point in buying equipment with good audio quality if all you have to play back through is a second-rate hi-fi system (Figure 2-2).

Whatever your total budget is for the system, allow at least 10% of it for the 'little' items, many of which are small in size but not in

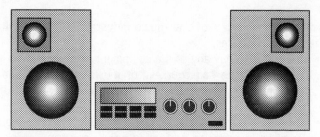

Figure 2-2 Is your hi-fi system good enough to listen through?

price! There are also countless of these that you will only think of when you actually start to put the system together. Some suggestions:

- Mains blocks (see Chapter 8).
- Audio patchbays, which save continuous recabling behind units and mixers.
- Main audio cabling; expensive to buy if you are setting up an 8/16 track studio, time consuming to make from cable and jack plugs.
- Audio and MIDI leads; lots of them, various different lengths.
- Blank disks for computers and samplers, preferably a brand name for reliability.
- Blank tape or cassettes for the multi-track, preferably the brand for which the machine has been set-up (usually mentioned in the manual).
- Paper and spare ribbons/cartridges for the printer.
- Cleaning kit and de-magnetizer for any tape recorders.
- Audio adaptors to connect any kind of audio in/out to your mixer.
- Footswitches for any synths or keyboards.
- Microphone pop guard.

Buying second-hand

A thorny issue, but one that must be addressed. Given a careful first user, almost anything can be bought second-hand, but some items are more susceptible to wear and damage than others. Running through the obvious ones:

- Sound module; no moving parts and easy to check. Have a look at the MIDI In socket and around the on/off switch. Wear in these places shows that the unit has been heavily used.
- Effects unit; again, no moving parts. If a unit has an external power supply, check whether the cables going into it are damaged as such power supplies are often expensive to replace.
- Dedicated sequencer; if it has a disk drive, listen to the level of noise when it is in use. While a high level might not necessarily mean that the drive is worn, remember that replacing disk drives is an expensive business.
- Computer; again, check the disk drive and have a careful look at the general condition. How dirty is the keyboard? This often gives a good indication as to age and use because keyboards are quite difficult to keep clean.
- Multi-track/cassette recorder; check the heads. They should be clean of tape residue and without any flat, worn surfaces. Record onto each track, play back and check the sound quality. Is there any 'warbling' of the sound?

Be very careful when buying anything involving moving parts such as a disk drive or tape heads. Replacement of worn items such as these is very expensive both in terms of the parts themselves and the labour costs. If the saving of a second-hand item over a new one is reasonably small, go for the new item every time. It is better to start the system with less equipment, all of which is functioning properly, than an entire system that keeps breaking down.

Using natural resources

Buying equipment, finding that it doesn't fit the bill and reselling it a few weeks later is tantamount to throwing money away. Mistakes where equipment is concerned are going to be expensive.

There are various ways that you can learn about the equipment you are proposing to buy:

- Read reviews in the various music magazines. You will soon find that there are certain reviewers who are on the same wavelength as you and place more weight on their comments.
- If there is a particular point that you don't quite understand, write to, or call, the magazine. If it's a salient point, the maga-

zine may print your letter and their reply. Always enclose a stamped-addressed envelope.

- Speak to friends and colleagues, but always remember that someone else's viewpoint will never quite match up with yours.
- If you cannot decide between, say, one of two items, contact the manufacturer or distributor and ask them to send you a photocopy of the manuals. There may be a small charge, but at least you will be able to pore over these and accurately compare the facilities and functions.
- Go to public music shows. Most of these are of the 'hands on' variety where you can try out a piece of equipment and put it through its paces. As most shows use headphones, be careful not to draw too many conclusions about the sound quality.
- Speak to other musicians and find out how good the music shops are in your area. Don't place complete importance on the lowest prices because after-sales support and breadth of selection are also important.
- Strike up a rapport with what you feel to be the best shop for you. Get to know the salesmen by name but without being labelled a pest! You are more likely to get straight answers to your questions and good deals on equipment you want to buy because shops go out of their way to keep good customers.

Buying items one at a time is a good idea because it gives you the chance to get to know a piece of equipment before moving onto the next item. If you buy an entire system in one go, you are less likely to be able to use any particular piece to its full capabilities. There is a certain charm in hunting around for individual items for a system, but this is not to everybody's taste and you may want to buy your entire system from one dealer. If that is the case, make certain that most of the 'little' items mentioned above are included, especially the audio cables, some blank tapes and a selection of MIDI leads.

Finally, remember the (slightly altered) old adage: Buy in haste, regret at leisure!

Cabling a basic MIDI system

MIDI cables

Nearly every piece of MIDI equipment has a MIDI In and a MIDI Out each as a 5-pin DIN socket. In fact, you have probably seen very similar sockets on a hi-fi amplifier or cassette deck. Without going into too much detail of how MIDI works, suffice to say that only three pins out of the five require connections (Figure 3-1). Pin 2 at one end of the

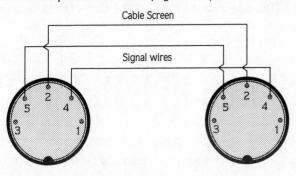

Figure 3-1 Only pins 2, 4 and 5 are used for MIDI connections

lead connects to pin 2 at the other end by the cable screen while pin 4 connects to pin 4 and pin 5 to pin 5, both being used for the MIDI signal.

There is generally nothing wrong with using MIDI cables that have all five pins connected and most cheap leads are of this type. Avoid using hi-fi leads as these often tend to have the pins connected in reverse and such a lead will not work at all with MIDI equipment. The general rule is to use the shortest leads possible to connect a system and if you have to use any long cabling because equipment is situated a distance apart, spend a little extra on such leads. Remember that many manufacturers now include a MIDI lead or two with their equipment, especially where synths are concerned. Before you go out and buy all the cables that you think you are going to need, check this as it may allow you to make a small saving.

In, Out and Thru

An understanding of the differences between MIDI In, Out and Thru sockets is essential if you are to be able to put a MIDI system together. A MIDI Out can be viewed as the 'mouth' of a MIDI device as any MIDI information created is transmitted from this socket. For instance, if you press a key on a keyboard, the information about that note is sent from the MIDI Out. A MIDI In can be similarly looked upon as the 'ears' because it is here that MIDI information is received. Continuing the above example, the keyboard MIDI Out may be connected to the MIDI In of a sound module. The note created by pressing a

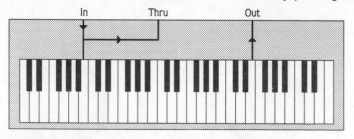

Figure 3-2 MIDI sockets on a standard synth keyboard.

key is transmitted from the MIDI Out on the keyboard and received at the MIDI In of the sound module.

A MIDI Thru provides a replica of the information received at the MIDI In socket so that it can be passed on to another MIDI device. If you like, this is like a next door neighbour who hears everything and then runs outside to inform the rest of the world! Figure 3-2 shows a MIDI In, Out and Thru on a keyboard; the arrows should give you a good idea of how the sockets are used.

As both a MIDI Thru and MIDI Out can send out MIDI information, this gives a basic rule for MIDI connections - a MIDI Thru or Out is always connected to a MIDI In. Worth remembering because connecting two MIDI Ins or Outs together cannot possibly work and may even cause damage.

Connecting a synth and a sound module

The most basic connection is that of a keyboard and an expander, or sound module. It may be that you already own a synth and wish to expand the sounds available from your system, or that you have purchased a master keyboard and intend to obtain the sounds from another unit. Either way, you need to connect the keyboard and sound module (Figure 3-3).

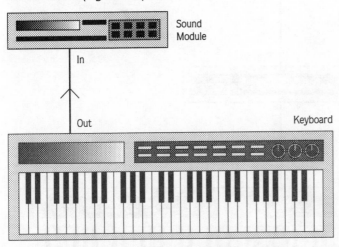

Figure 3-3 Connecting an expander to a synth keyboard

The MIDI Out from the synth connects to the MIDI In of the expander so that the 'mouth' is connected to the 'ears'. The synth will then be set to transmit on one of the 16 available MIDI channels and the expander must be set to receive information on the same MIDI channel. Pressing keys on the synth or using the modulation or pitch bend wheels will then send out information that the expander can react to.

Connecting multiple sound modules

You may decide later that you wish to add another expander to further broaden the number of sounds available to your system. Alternatively, you may have made that decision at the very beginning and started your system with two or more sound modules and a master keyboard. Connections now require the use of the MIDI Thru socket (Figure 3-4).

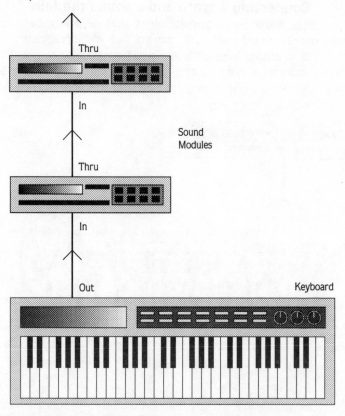

Figure 3-4 Using a MIDI Thru to connect multiple sound modules

As the MIDI Thru socket carries a copy of all information received at the MIDI In, any information received by the first sound module will also be received by the second one. This manner of connecting MIDI devices is usually called a 'daisy chain' and can be extended to further expanders.

Devices without a MIDI Thru

When MIDI was first designed, the idea of a MIDI Thru socket was not mentioned and so some early synths and sound modules do not have one. Also, as a cost-cutting exercise, it is not unusual to find that some budget devices are lacking in this area as well, especially where

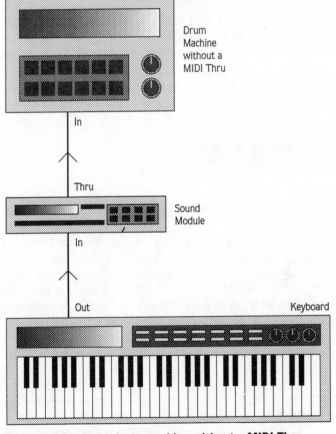

Figure 3-5 Placing a drum machine without a MIDI Thru at the end of a daisy chain

drum machines are concerned. If this is the case with a piece of equipment that you have bought, then it has to be connected at the end of the chain (Figure 3-5).

Using a MIDI Thru box

A great deal has been written about so-called 'MIDI delays' being caused by having a MIDI daisy chain containing several devices. The idea is that it takes time for the MIDI signal to be duplicated upon being received at the MIDI In and sent out again from the MIDI Thru. This is not true! By the very design of MIDI, it should take less than 2 microseconds for this to happen - 2 millionths of a second. It takes nearly 500 times longer to transfer a note over MIDI!

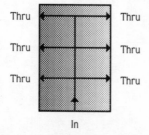

Figure 3-6 MIDI Thru box

The MIDI signal can degrade as it is continually copied. Ultimately, this will lead to it becoming unrecognisable by a MIDI device and so information could get lost. For example, an expander may not get the information to turn a note off which would then be left 'hanging'. A further inconvenience is that you have to remember to switch on every piece of equipment in the chain as MIDI Thru sockets cannot function without the MIDI device being turned on. So even though you only want to use the first and last out of, say, six items, all have to be powered up.

The way around this is to use a MIDI Thru box (Figure 3-6). This rather inexpensive piece of equipment takes a single MIDI In and duplicates it several times.

A MIDI Thru box can be used to eradicate the continuous connecting of MIDI Thru to MIDI In from one device to the next. It is also

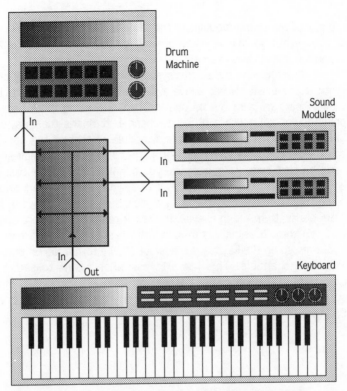

Figure 3-7 Creating a star system with a MIDI Thru box

useful for connecting more than one device without a MIDI Thru to your system (Figure 3-7) and is usually called a 'star' system.

MIDI information is transmitted from the MIDI Out of the synth and received by the MIDI In of the Thru box. Here it is duplicated and sent on to any connected devices where it is received and acted upon.

Using multiple sound modules

The use of this system is the same whether you are using the daisy chain or star arrangement of connection. The method of connection simply depends on the number of MIDI devices and the convenience of connection to a central point.

The immediate use of more than one sound module is to double up on sounds to make them richer and fuller. Set the MIDI receive

21

channel of the sound modules to the same as the transmit MIDI channel of your synth so that any key pressed on the synth will have all the sound modules playing as well.

A second way to use this system is to use a split facility on your synth if one exists. Notes above a particular key on one MIDI channel (upper split) are sent out on one MIDI channel while those below that point (lower split) use a different channel. If this is the case, set the MIDI receive channel on one sound module to that of the upper split and the other to the lower split. This then allows you to play different parts on each synth. For instance, you might have a double bass sound being played on the lower split by one synth and the lead brass line being played on the upper split by a second expander. With the sounds from the synth mixed in as well, the result can be quite impressive.

A third possibility is if your synth has a dual mode where every note pressed on the keyboard sends out MIDI information on two different MIDI channels. This leads to a similar result to setting two expanders to the same MIDI channel, but also lets you call up different sounds on each expander independently by using MIDI Program Changes.

4

Fitting a sequencer into the system

Different kinds of sequencer

Any device that records MIDI information can effectively be called a sequencer, the term being a throwback to the days when some synths had a small memory of, perhaps, 16 steps that could be played 'in sequence'. A modern-day sequencer records all MIDI information that appears at its MIDI In socket. For instance, a synth connected to a sequencer will send out information about the keys pressed, when you let the keys go, when you move the pitch bend or modulation wheels and so on.

It is very important to understand that only the information about your 'performance' is being recorded, not the actual sounds. When the sequencer is played back, the recorded information is sent out from

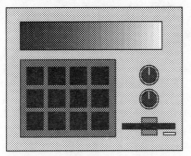

Figure 4-1 Dedicated sequencers often have the useful feature of a disk drive

the MIDI Out and received at the MIDI In of the synth or sound module at which point the data is translated into a repeat performance.

There are three different kinds of sequencer. The first is the stand-alone, dedicated type in a box (Figure 4-1) that usually has a small screen, a disadvantage when it comes to editing, and may or may not have a disk drive for saving songs to. Older sequencers, and some modern budget versions, often need to be connected to a tape recorder to save the data for songs to tape, a slow and unreliable method.

The second type of sequencer is a program running on a computer (Figure 4-2). While this has a large screen for editing, it is hardly

Figure 4-2 Most computers now have sequencing programs available. The screen is a big advantage where editing is concerned

portable and you have to get to know the way the computer works before being able to use the sequencing program.

The final type is incorporated into a synth and tends to be called a 'workstation'. This has the advantage of portability, which is especially relevant where live work is concerned, but the sequencing side is often compromised by the price and so lacking in functions. Of course, a workstation does remove the problem of cabling the sequencer into the MIDI system!

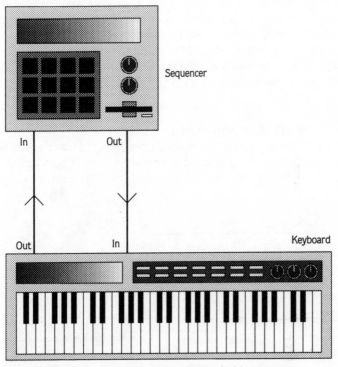

Figure 4-3 A two-way connection is needed between a synth and sequencer

Sequencer and synth system

Taking the most basic set-up of a sequencer and a synth, the connection is a two-way affair with each MIDI Out being connected to the other's MIDI In (Figure 4-3).

MIDI information from the synth is sent out from the synth's MIDI Out, received at the MIDI In of the sequencer and recorded. On play-back, the information is sent from the sequencer's MIDI Out back to the synth's MIDI In and the original performance is reproduced.

If the synth can only play a single sound at a time, then the usefulness of this set-up is limited. Take the example of wanting a backing of piano and bass. If the synth is set to a bass sound, you can play the bass line that you want and record it onto a track of the sequencer. On play-back, that bass line will be reproduced. Now change to a piano sound. To be able to record the second track on the sequencer, you need to hear the bass line from the first track. However, you cannot do that any longer because the sound on the synth is now a piano one!

Multi-timbral synth

What is needed is a multi-timbral synth. This is one which can play many different sounds at the same time, with each sound usually given a different MIDI channel. However, the MIDI transmit channel for

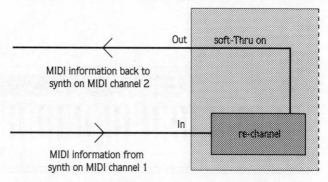

Figure 4-4 Sequencers use a 'soft-thru' facility to save you having to continually change the MIDI transmit channel of the synth

the synth usually remains the same as most sequencers allow you to assign a MIDI channel to the current track you are recording on. The MIDI channel of received MIDI information is then changed to this MIDI channel and retransmitted it from the MIDI Out. This is usually known as rechanneling and requires the sequencer facility of 'soft-thru' to be turned on (Figure 4-4).

Try looking at the above example again. Let's say that the synth is transmitting on MIDI channel 1 and that MIDI channel 1 is being used for the bass sound and MIDI channel 2 for the piano sound. For the first recording, the bass track, the MIDI channel for this track is set to 1 and the line is recorded on the sequencer. For the piano part, the MIDI channel for track 2 is set to 2 and so allows you to hear the bass line playing back on your synth while you are recording the piano part.

Do you see a possible problem? There is one, and it occurs when you are recording the bass part. Playing the synth creates the bass sound that you hear. However, the MIDI information enters the

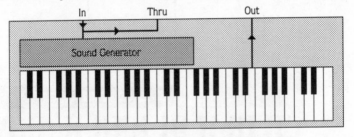

Figure 4-5 A keyboard with a Local Control Off facility works by separating the keys from the sounds

sequencer which then sends it back out to the synth again. This results in you hearing the bass line twice, the second time being a fraction of a second after the first. To get around this, most synths now support a facility called Local Control Off (commonly referred to simply as 'Local Off') where the internal sounds are effectively divorced from the keys and so playing the keyboard does not actually generate any sound (Figure 4-5).

Sequencers and sound modules

From the previous chapter, we saw that there are two ways of connecting MIDI devices to a MIDI system; daisy chain and star arrangement. This is equally true when a sequencer is incorporated into the system (Figures 4-6 and 4-7).

Either of these methods will work satisfactorily provided that the number of MIDI devices is small, say four. Beyond this, the MIDI signal may be corrupted as mentioned in the last chapter. If you are going

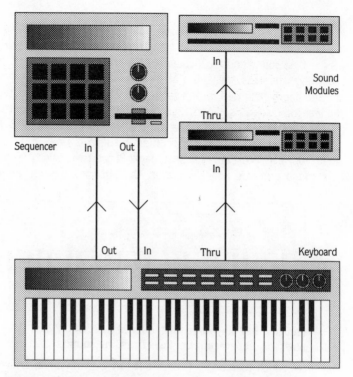

Figure 4-6 Using a daisy chain system with a sequencer

to buy a MIDI Thru box, don't make the mistake of buying one with just enough Thrus for your current set-up; allow for a few more to save you the expense of having to buy another Thru box later.

More than one MIDI Out

What happens if you have two multi-timbral expanders, each of which can support 16 instruments playing on 16 MIDI channels? With only a single MIDI Out, you only have access to 16 MIDI channels.

Some dedicated sequencers have more than one MIDI Out, and many computer-based sequencers can support a small add-on box with extra MIDI Outs. These MIDI Outs might simply work together as the equivalent of MIDI Thrus, in which case you are still limited to 16 MIDI channels. If they function independently, you effectively have multiples of 16 MIDI channels (Figure 4-8).

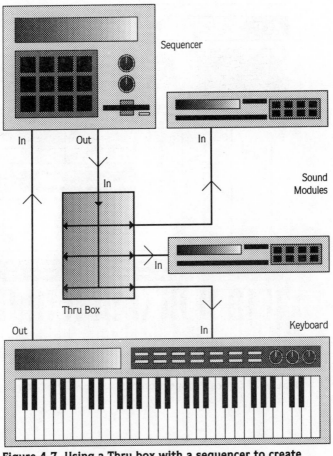

Figure 4-7 Using a Thru box with a sequencer to create a star arrangement

If you intend to use several expanders, it is worth looking for a sequencer that has more than one MIDI Out. Apart from the advantage of being able to use more than 16 instruments, extra MIDI Outs also simplify the cabling of a system as less MIDI Thrus have to be used.

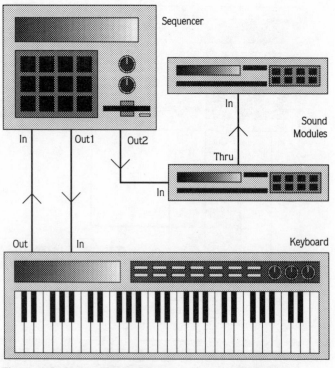

**Figure 4-8 A sequencer with more than one indepen-
dent MIDI Out can support more than 16 MIDI channels**

5

Switchers and mergers

What is a MIDI switcher?

If you have worked with a mixer and tape recorder, there will probably have been a time when you were short of an input. Perhaps you simply spliced together a couple of audio leads to get around the problem. While strictly speaking you should also use a few resistors to construct a basic mixer circuit, you can often get away without this. MIDI is a very different animal and cable splicing is most definitely a no-no.

Why might you want two MIDI Outs to share the same MIDI In? A typical example is when you are using two or more MIDI controllers in your MIDI system. This is not unreasonable as you may have a keyboard for synth parts and a drum machine for rhythm parts. Many drum machines send out MIDI information when you hit the pads and so drum parts can be played on the drum machine, recorded on a sequencer and then sent back to the drum machine on play-back. This is effectively using the drum machine as a controller to record MIDI information with, and as a drum sound module for play-back (Figure 5-1), hence the connection from the MIDI Thru of the synth to the MIDI In of the drum machine.

As you only need one controller at a time, you could simply plug and unplug the lead from the MIDI Out of the relevant controller to the MIDI In of the sequencer as necessary. However, this is hardly an ideal situation. A much better idea is to use a MIDI switcher.

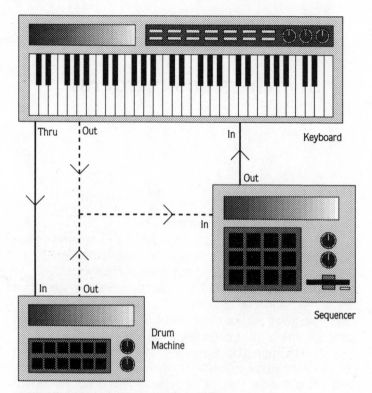

Thru   Out   In   Keyboard

Out

In

In   Out

Sequencer

Drum
Machine

Figure 5-1 If you want to use two MIDI controllers, you have to recable your system each time you change between them

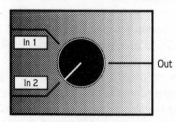

In 1

In 2

Out

Figure 5-2 A typical two in, one out MIDI switcher

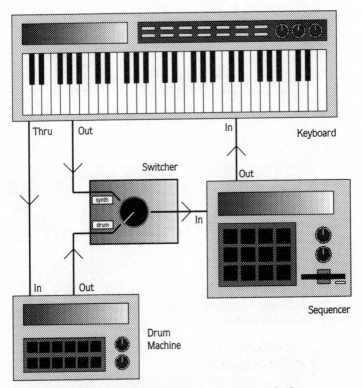

Figure 5-3 Using a MIDI switcher is an elegant solution to using two MIDI controllers

Using a MIDI switcher

A MIDI switcher, or MIDI switch box as it is sometimes called, is a unit that lets you select which of several inputs is connected to the output. It normally uses a rotary switch to select one of the MIDI Ins and direct it to its output (Figure 5-2). Such a device is passive in that it does not require power and so is cheap to buy.

Using a MIDI switcher, you no longer have to recable the system each time you want to change to the other MIDI controller (Figure 5-3). When the switch points upwards, the synth is the current controller and you can play in parts via the keys. When the switch points downwards, the drum machine becomes the controller and the rhythm parts can

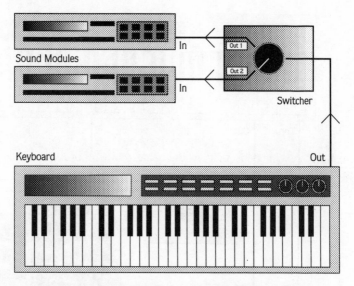

Figure 5-4 Using a MIDI switcher the other way round allows you to choose between two sounds modules when playing live

then be played in via the pads. More about working with a drum machine in the next chapter.

A MIDI switcher has another important use for live musicians in that it allows you to choose between different expanders. By using the switches the other way round, you can select which of two (or more) MIDI Ins the MIDI Out of the synth is connected to (Figure 5-4).

Using a MIDI switcher in this way is easier than having to turn the level down on each module as you move from one to the other. However, take care not to switch between them while notes are still playing. This will result in hanging notes as an expander fails to get the MIDI information to turn off the notes that are playing.

What is a MIDI merger?

The point of using a MIDI switcher is to allow you to select which of two, or more, MIDI controllers is the active one at a particular time. However, you do not get the option to use both at the same time. Why might you wish to do so? From a live point of view, you

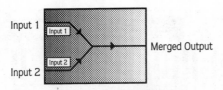

Figure 5-5 A standard MIDI merger

might need to share a sound module or MIDI system with another play-er. For instance, one person could play a keyboard while the other might use drum pads to play the same multi-timbral sound module, each using a different sound.

A MIDI merger is a device that combines the MIDI information from two MIDI Outs, and requires a degree of intelligence to do so (Figure 5-5). Consequently a micro-processor has to be used. MIDI messages often consist of two or three parts and it is important to ensure that all parts of a message are kept together; if this is not so, the message becomes garbled. Consequently, a MIDI merger is far more expensive than a MIDI Thru box or switcher.

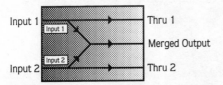

Figure 5-6 A MIDI merger with MIDI Thrus for the two MIDI Ins

There is a second type of MIDI merger, one that has MIDI Thrus for each of the two inputs (Figure 5-6) and this can be useful for live applications. Figure 5.8 later in this chapter covers such a merger.

Using a MIDI merger

A common use for a MIDI merger is in the way described above; two people with different MIDI controllers playing the same sound module (Figure 5-7).

In the example, drum pads and a keyboard are both playing a multi-timbral sound module. The MIDI transmit channels for the two controllers must be set to different values to play different instruments

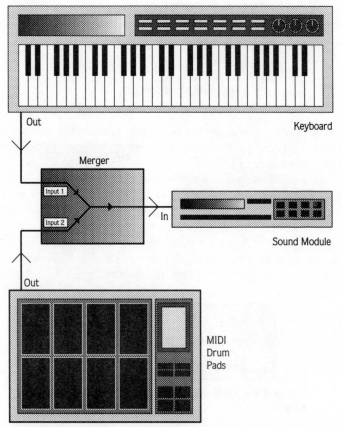

Figure 5-7 Two MIDI controllers playing the same sound module

independently of one another. Of course, care has to be taken to ensure that one controller does not play so many notes as to exceed the polyphony of the expander!

For live applications, a MIDI merger of the second type is useful in that each player can have their own individual sound module as well as sharing one (Figure 5-8).

In this case, the two individual sound modules being used by each player do not need to be multi-timbral, but could be set to receive on a different MIDI channel from the shared module. By changing the MIDI transmit channel of the controller, a player could decide which

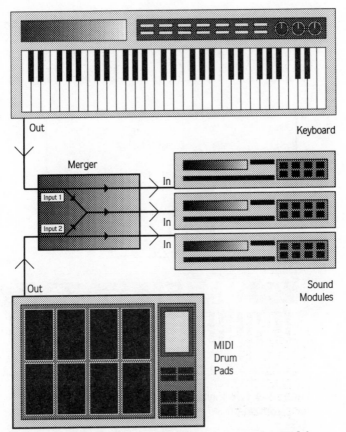

**Figure 5-8 A MIDI merger with MIDI Thrus can be useful
for live applications**

module to play. Alternatively, the individual sound module could be set
to the same MIDI channel as the shared module and sounds doubled up.

A very simple way to use a MIDI Merger live is to share a synth
that has a Local Control Off facility (Figure 5-9).

If you recall from the previous chapter, Local Control Off splits
the sounds from the keyboard in a synth. So two keyboards can share
the sounds from one synth by merging their MIDI Outs and sending this
to the MIDI In.

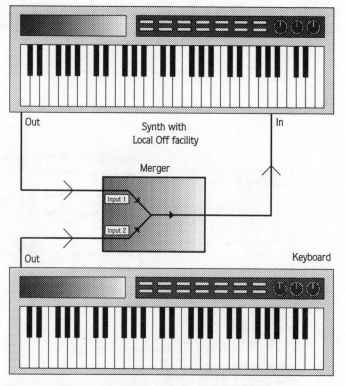

Figure 5-9 Two keyboards sharing a synth by using local control off

Voice editing

There is one particular situation where a MIDI merger is invaluable and that is when you are using a computer to edit the sounds of an expander. As the expander lacks a keyboard, it is impossible to hear the changes to the sounds in a proper context. Many voice editing programs give you an on-screen keyboard, but using a mouse to click on a screen figure is very different from seeing how a sound reacts when played from a keyboard.

A two-way connection between the computer and expander is necessary. The computer has to ask for all parameters to be sent to it so that it has a precise picture of the current sounds and set-up of the expander and does this by sending a MIDI message from its MIDI Out to

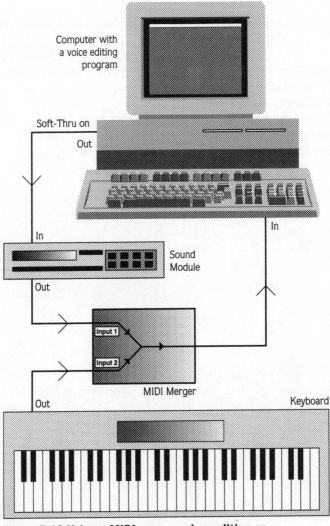

Figure 5-10 Using a MIDI merger when editing an expander's sounds

the MIDI In of the expander. The expander then needs to send the information to the computer which it does via its MIDI Out to the MIDI In of the computer. If both MIDI Ins and Outs are in use, how can a keyboard by integrated into the system? This is where a MIDI merger comes in (Figure 5-10).

When you want to hear the current sound, playing the keyboard will send notes to the computer via the MIDI merger. The computer will then send the notes out from its MIDI Out, using a soft-Thru, and the expander will receive them.

If the expander is multi-timbral, the voice editing program will have the facility to rechannel the notes so that you always hear the part being edited - there is little point in hearing the wrong sound!

6

Drum machines

Working with a drum machine

Working within a MIDI system, there are three ways that you can use a drum machine:

- As a sound module purely for its drum sounds, being played by a sequencer.
- As a controller by tapping the rhythms on the pads and recording the MIDI information on a sequencer. On play-back it behaves as a sound module.
- To program rhythms on the drum machine and then make it play back in time with the sequencer on which the rest of a song has been recorded.

Using a drum machine as a sound module

While there are sound modules around which are dedicated to drum sounds, it is very common to purchase a drum machine with no intention to use the internal sequencer. The most obvious reason for this is that you already have a dedicated sequencer, either as a stand-alone unit or in the way of a computer program.

To be able to use a drum machine as a sound module, you need to 'play' the drum sounds. There are two common ways of doing this. The first is via the step input facility on the sequencer which allows you to say what note you want played and when. While this is often well catered for on a computer sequencer where such things can be shown visually, it is often more difficult to step-enter drums on a stand-alone sequencer. The second way to access the drum sounds is via a key-

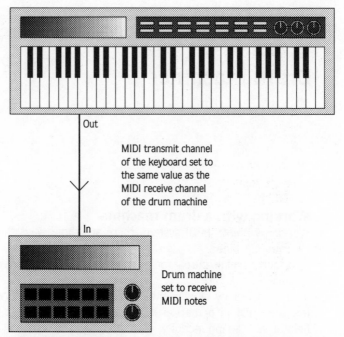

Figure 6-1 Playing the sounds in a drum machine via a MIDI keyboard

board. Connect the MIDI Out of the keyboard to the MIDI In of the drum machine and the audio outputs of this to a hi-fi or audio system (Figure 6-1).

To hear the sounds, the drum machine must be set to receive MIDI notes. Usually, there is a list of the default numbers of the MIDI notes in the back of the manual. The lowest note on a MIDI keyboard is typically MIDI Note number 36, but you can soon find out by pressing this key and seeing which sound it plays. Any keyboard will do, even a cheap four-octave one that you wouldn't use for anything else - you could quite happily mark the names of the drum sounds on each key. If you don't hear anything, check the MIDI transmit channel of the keyboard and the MIDI receive channel of the drum machine, which should be the same.

Apart from just hearing the drum sounds, you are also likely to want to record your key presses on a sequencer (Figure 6-2).

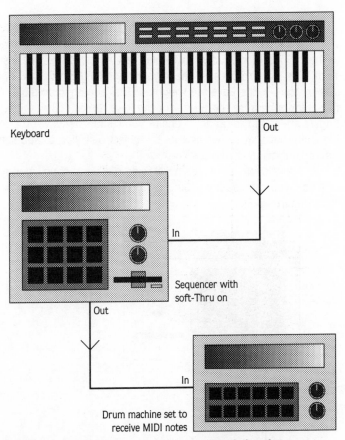

Keyboard

Out

In

Sequencer with
soft-Thru on

Out

In

Drum machine set to
receive MIDI notes

Figure 6-2 Recording drum rhythms, played via a keyboard, on a sequencer

Connecting the MIDI Out of the keyboard to the MIDI In of the sequencer allows the sequencer to record any key presses you make. The MIDI Out of the sequencer is then connected to the MIDI In of the drum machine which is set to receive MIDI notes. This time, you do not need to be concerned with the MIDI transmit channel of the keyboard because you can use the rechanneling feature of the sequencer to set the MIDI channel accordingly. You will want to hear the drum sounds while you record the key presses on the sequencer, so the soft-Thru facility must be turned on.

Using a drum machine as a MIDI controller

Various problems occur when playing a drum machine via a keyboard. It's often awkward to play fast rhythms like, for instance, a 16th hihat pattern because the keys are too small to fit two fingers on side by side. If the keys are weighted, it is almost impossible to play a fast rhythm because the weight of the keys forces them up just as your fingers are trying to go down again! You could slow down the tempo of the song, but that rather defeats the object of trying to add some realism to your drum rhythms.

Many drum machines have large pads and if you purchase one of these, you can use the drum machine as a MIDI controller in its own right (Figure 6-3).

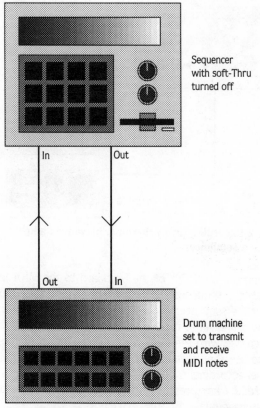

Sequencer
with soft-Thru
turned off

In   Out

Out   In

Drum machine
set to transmit
and receive
MIDI notes

Figure 6-3 Using a drum machine as a MIDI controller

The drum machine must be set to both transmit and receive MIDI notes, and the soft-Thru facility of the sequencer must be turned off. This is because drum machines generally do not have a Local Control Off feature and so you will hear the drum sound once when you hit the pad and again when it is returned via the soft-Thru. If pressing play on the sequencer automatically triggers off the drum

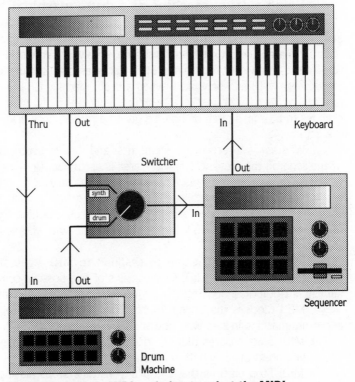

Figure 6-4 Using a MIDI switcher to select the MIDI controller for the system

machine's internal sequencer, this means that the sequencer is sending out a timing message called MIDI Clock. Find a function called 'Send MIDI Sync' or similar and turn it off.

If you want to alternate between a drum machine and a keyboard as the MIDI controller for the system, it is useful to use a MIDI switcher as covered in the last chapter (Figure 6-4).

Such a set-up is very neat. A flick of a switch lets you change between the drum machine and the synth as the main MIDI controller while the rest of the connections ensure that you can hear both the synth and drum sounds.

Using a drum machine as a drum machine!

Having purchased a computer and sequencing program, why on earth would you want to program drums on a drum machine? Two possible reasons, the first being that you simply prefer working that way! Also, some drum machines offer facilities that cannot be controlled over MIDI and only work when a drum machine is playing back its own patterns. For instance, a drum machine might make slight changes to a drum's pitch or tone so giving a rather more 'live' feel to the pattern.

Whether you record the drums first and then structure the rest of the song on the sequencer or vice versa is up to you. Ultimately, you will need to get the drum machine and sequencer playing in time with each other. This is usually called synchronisation or sync for short. The sequencer sends out sync information and the drum machine responds to this by starting, stopping and playing in time with the sequencer (Figure 6-5).

Set the drum machine to respond to MIDI sync and the sequencer to transmit it. MIDI sync consists of five possible commands namely MIDI Clock, Start, Stop, Continue and Song Position Pointer.

MIDI Clock is the timing information that keeps the sequencer and drum machine in step with one another.

- MIDI Start ensures that the drum machine starts to play when you press the play button on the sequencer.
- MIDI Stop ensures that the drum machine stops playing when you press the stop button on the sequencer.
- MIDI Continue acts as a pause control. If you press stop followed by play on the sequencer, the drum machine will continue from where it previously halted.
- Song Position Pointer allows a drum machine to start from a place other than the beginning of a song. Starting the sequencer at, say, bar 10 will start the drum machine from the same place.

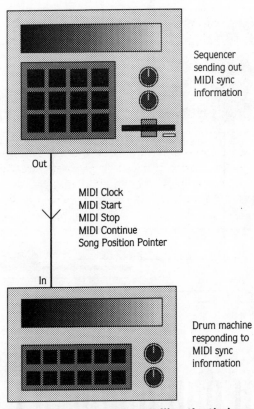

Sequencer
sending out
MIDI sync
information

Out

MIDI Clock
MIDI Start
MIDI Stop
MIDI Continue
Song Position Pointer

In

Drum machine
responding to
MIDI sync
information

**Figure 6-5 Sequencer controlling the timing of a drum
machine by using MIDI sync**

Not all sequencers transmit all of these commands, and not all
drum machines respond to them. MIDI Clock and MIDI Start are always
used, but what difference does it make if some of the others are not
transmitted or recognised? No MIDI Stop means that the drum
machine will carry on playing when the sequencer is stopped. No MIDI
Continue means that the drum machine will always go back to the
beginning of the song whenever the sequencer is paused. No Song
Position Pointer means that the drum machine always starts from the
beginning of the song, irrespective of where you start the sequencer.

The rest of the system can be put together, with or without a
MIDI Thru box as before (Figure 6-6).

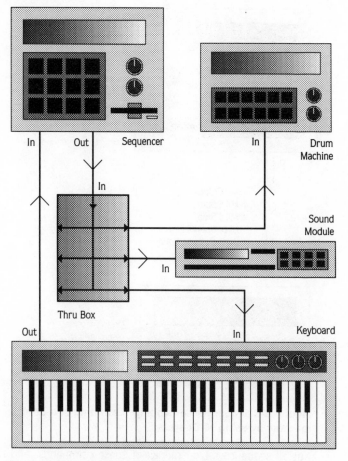

Figure 6-6 Complete MIDI system of sequencer and drum machine, with the sequencer acting as the timing master

While the MIDI sync information is also received by the other devices in the system, they will not respond to the messages unless they contain a sequencer which, except for a workstation, is unlikely. If your synth is also a workstation, select the function that makes it respond to MIDI sync and turn it off.

It is possible that you have a drum machine with better MIDI sync facilities than your sequencer! If this is the case, you could always make

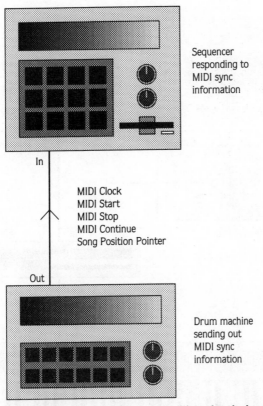

Figure 6-7 Drum machine controlling the timing of a sequencer by using MIDI sync

the drum machine the timing master (Figure 6-7). However, if the MIDI In of the sequencer is taken up in this manner, you cannot connect a keyboard as well without using a MIDI Merger (Figure 6-8). The note and performance information from the synth will be merged with the MIDI sync information from the drum machine and sent to the sequencer. While this will work fine, use the original method if possible as it is less complicated and cheaper due to the lack of the MIDI merger.

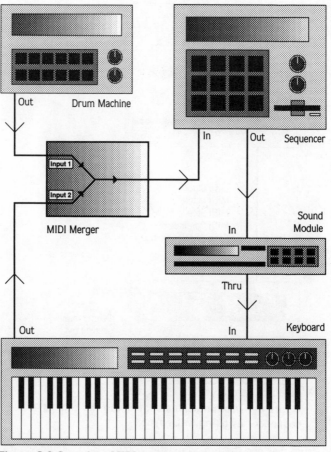

Figure 6-8 Complete MIDI system of sequencer and drum machine, with the drum machine acting as the timing master

7

Sequencers and multi-track tape recorders

MIDI, multi-track recorder or both?

A MIDI sequencer is a very powerful tool, both in the studio and live. With just the basic 16 MIDI channels it can control 16 different instruments, effectively allowing you to play back most of an entire musical piece. However, a MIDI sequencer does not record actual sound. When you hear an expander playing an authentic piano, the piano sound has been digitally recorded and placed in a chip in the expander's circuitry. While any sound can be recorded digitally and so treated in a similar way to MIDI, suffice to say that such devices are expensive and beyond the scope of this book.

So what do we use to record vocals and real instruments? The perennial multi-track recorder! This has between 4 and 24 tracks typically and the tape can take many different formats; cassette, reel to reel, cartridge and so on. Most budget multi-tracks offer four or eight tracks on cassette or eight tracks on reel-to-reel with 1/4 or 1/2 tape.

What disadvantage does a budget multi-track have? The main one is the limited number of tracks, but this can be helped by using a sequencer in tandem with the recorder. Synth and drum machine sounds need not be recorded to tape but the two systems have to keep time with one another. In theprevious chapter, we saw that a drum machine and sequencer can be kept in time by using MIDI sync. A similar process is used here.

Using tape sync

The most basic method to keep a multi-track recorder and a MIDI sequencer in sync is to use a tape sync box (Figure 7-1). This converts the MIDI Clock messages sent out from the sequencer into a special tone (called FSK for Frequency Shift Keying) which can be record-

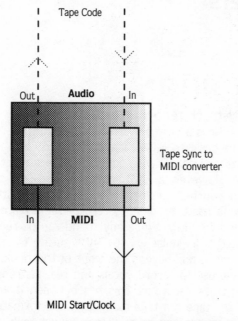

Figure 7-1 A tape sync to MIDI converter records the sequencer's timing information as a code on tape

ed onto tape. On play-back, the tone is converted back into MIDI Clocks for the sequencer to stay in time with the recorder (Figure 7-2). This, of course, means the loss of one track on the recorder.

How do you work with a tape sync to MIDI converter?

- Complete the song on the sequencer including any tempo or time signature changes.
- Set the sequencer to transmit MIDI Clock.
- Prepare the recorder to record on the outermost track (that is, track 8 on an eight track recorder or track 4 on a four track) with a level of about -3dB.

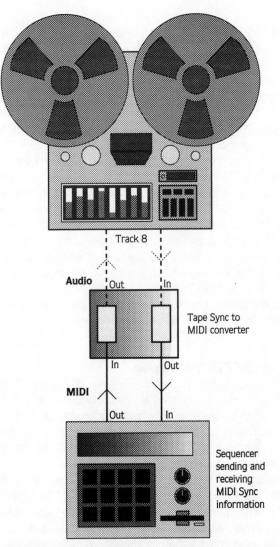

Track 8

Audio

Out   In

Tape Sync to
MIDI converter

In   Out

MIDI

Out   In

Sequencer
sending and
receiving
MIDI Sync
information

**Figure 7-2 Using a tape sync to MIDI converter to run a
multi-track recorder and sequencer in sync**

- Start recording on the multi-track.
- Start the tape sync to MIDI converter.
- Wait about 10 seconds and then set the sequencer to play.

It is important to leave the 10 second gap so that the tape signal can settle down. When the song finishes, all three devices can be stopped.

On play-back, the sequencer is set to receive MIDI sync and the tape recorder is set to play. The tape Sync to MIDI converter receives the tone from tape and sends out a MIDI Start to set the sequencer on its merry way. This is then followed up with MIDI Clocks to keep the recorder and sequencer in time with each other.

There is one problem. What happens if you start the tape part way into the song? The tape Sync to MIDI converter will still send out a MIDI Start and so the sequencer will always commence from the beginning of the song. To get around this there is a more modern version of FSK called Smart FSK. This encodes Song Position Pointers into the tape code as well so that you can start the song wherever you like on the tape recorder - the sequencer will always go to the correct place. Don't worry too much about the technicalities. Simply be aware of the procedure you have to follow to get the two machines to play in time with one another. Check your sequencer and make sure that you turn on Song Position Pointer if such an option exists.

Using SMPTE time code

SMPTE? An acronym for the Society of Motion Picture and Television Engineers who created a special type of tape sync that is now named after them. The important difference between this and FSK is that you don't have to run the sequencer when you record the tone. This means that you can record the code on the entire reel, a procedure commonly called 'striping' the tape.

There are two different types of SMPTE to MIDI converter (Figure 7-3). The first is very similar to the Smart FSK type in that it creates MIDI Start, Clock and Song Position Pointer messages. As the sequencer is not run when the code is recorded onto tape, you have to enter any tempo or time signature changes via a keypad on the unit which is rather awkward. The second type creates a different MIDI message called MIDI Time Code, or MTC for short, and the problem with tempo and time signature changes is no longer a problem. If your sequencer gives you the option, use MTC.

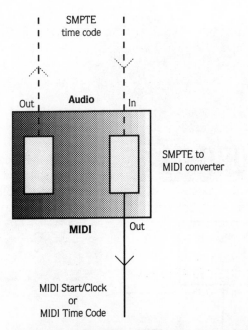

Figure 7-3 A SMPTE to MIDI converter outputs MIDI Clock and Start commands or MIDI Time Code

Putting the system together

The most difficult MIDI cabling problems invariably occur with tape sync boxes because they need access to one or both of the MIDI sockets of the sequencer. If you are using an FSK or Smart FSK box, the MIDI Out of the sequencer has to be connected to the MIDI In of the converter when the code is being recorded to tape. However, the MIDI Out of the tape sync box has to be connected to the MIDI In of the sequencer whenever the tape recorder is playing, to keep the sequencer in time with it. Some tape sync boxes have an extra MIDI In and an internal MIDI merger which can be used to combine keyboard information with the MIDI sync messages being internally created (Figure 7-4).

The keyboard's MIDI Thru is used to good effect here. When recording the tape sync, the sequencer's timing data is sent from the MIDI Out of the sequencer to the MIDI In of the keyboard and then via the MIDI Thru to the MIDI In of the tape sync converter. During play-

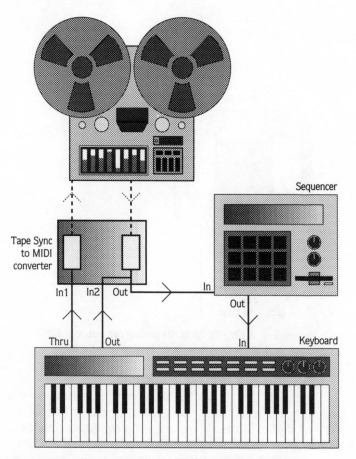

Figure 7-4 Some tape sync boxes have an extra MIDI In which can be used to merge the keyboard information with the MIDI sync data

back, the sequencer plays the synth and the recording of any extra sequencer tracks can occur due to the merging of keyboard information with the tape sync converter's MIDI sync data via the extra MIDI In on the converter. If no extra MIDI In exists, MIDI information has to be merged externally by using a separate MIDI mßerger (Figure 7-5).

Cabling a SMPTE to MIDI converter into the system is a very similar process. The only difference is that there is no need to worry

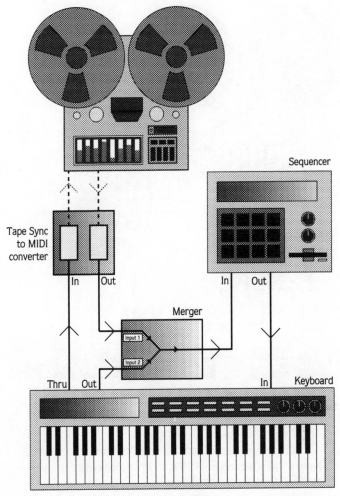

Figure 7-5 If there is no extra MIDI In on the tape sync converter, a MIDI merger is necessary

about routing the timing information from the sequencer to the SMPTE to MIDI box as it is not required. Again there are two types, one with a MIDI In to merge keyboard information with timing data (Figure 7-6), and one without (Figure 7-7).

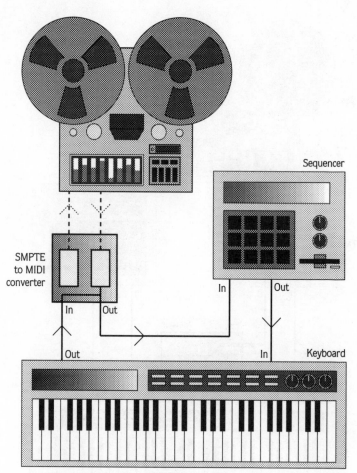

Figure 7-6 Cabling a SMPTE to MIDI converter is an easier task than a tape sync one

Using MIDI machine control

MIDI machine control (MMC) is a part of MIDI that allows sequencers to remotely control tape recorders. Moving the sequencer to, say, bar 20 sends out a MIDI command to the recorder instructing it to move to the same position. Once reached, the recorder enters play, sends out timing information and the sequencer starts to play in time.

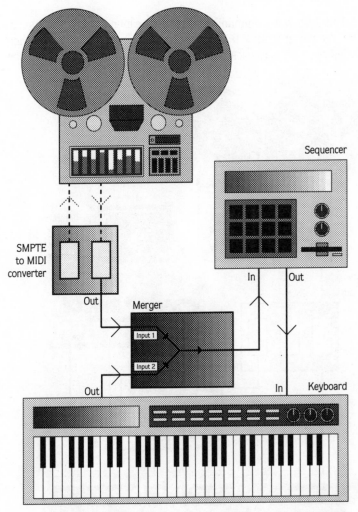

Figure 7-7 The lack of a merging MIDI In on the SMPTE to MIDI converter will require the use of a separate MIDI merger

This two-way communication makes cabling rather awkward. An MMC converter uses SMPTE to record time code to tape, and then reads this code on play-back. It also has a separate connection to the

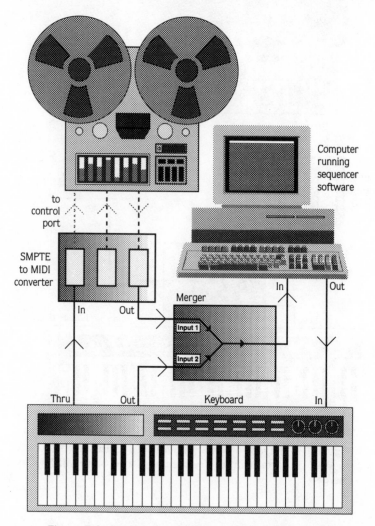

Figure 7-8 Cabling for a MIDI machine control system

recorder (control port) in order to convert the MIDI instructions from the sequencer into a form the recorder can understand (Figure 7-8).

Such a system grants you much freedom away from the recorder although only computer-based sequencers are likely to use MMC.

8

Practical setting up

Rack-mounted equipment

Working with music often requires inspiration which is easier to come by in a relaxed studio atmosphere. Crawling around on all fours trying to work out which plug has just blown a fuse, or putting your wrists through contortions while trying to find that spare MIDI Thru socket on the rear of a piece of equipment does not engender relaxation! Some thought needs to go into the way in which you position the equipment you buy.

Most MIDI equipment is of the rackmounting variety. It has a standard width and the height is generally measured as number of 'U's. The best way to site such equipment is in a rack which is a frame with mounting holes in the front to which you can attach your equipment via four screws. Racks tend to come in three varieties:

- Flight-cased. Such racks have lids front and back and are built to cope with being moved around by the live musician. Capacity varies between 1U and 10U typically.
- Floor-standing. As the name suggests, these are intended to be placed on the ground. Can be static (large capacity of 30U and more) or on wheels with the angle of the rack part being adjustable.
- Surface-standing. Smaller than the floor-standing variety and less robust but with a capacity usually between 4U and 12U typically.

If you are intending to use equipment in the studio and live, flight-cased racks are essential. If equipment is to be sited purely in the studio, floor or table standing racks will suffice. If you decide to use table racks, be careful what you put them on top of as several MIDI devices in a rack can be pretty heavy - many a table or shelf has collapsed under the weight!

Siting equipment

Look at most pieces of rackmounting MIDI equipment and you will see ventilation slots on either the top of the unit or underneath. The idea of these ventilation slots is to allow air to circulate within the piece of equipment and so keep it cool, a necessity when a device has a built-in mains transformer. Respect this point when siting such equipment in a rack and leave a space between units that have ventilation slots or else run the very real risk of overheating. If equipment with ventilation slots is to be left free-standing, make sure that the slots are left unobstructed. While it is very inviting to pile papers and other items on top, if the ventilation slots are there, leave them free. As for standing drinks on top of them...

Access is another important factor. The scenario at the beginning of this chapter of crawling on the floor and having to reach into awkward places is a very real one - this author has fallen into the trap before now! Rear access is essential, for while you believe that your installation is perfect it will most certainly break down at some point in the future and invariably when you can least afford it to do so. Being able to see all rear connections makes trouble-shooting far easier to carry out. This can be achieved by either having all racks and equipment on wheels and so mobile, or by leaving sufficient space behind equipment to be able to move in the gap.

Having access from the front seems obvious. After all, the equipment is facing you and you can reach the various on/off switches and front panel buttons. Many MIDI devices require you to carry out repetitive tasks such as clicking on buttons or turning data wheels and this can be a most uncomfortable procedure if you are, for example, kneeling down all the time. If you are working with a chair of some type in your studio, make sure that any device that requires you to do more than just turn it on and off is at a height that you can comfortably work with, and this includes the computer and monitor if you are using one. Regarding seats, that little bit extra spent on a typist's chair with wheels for the sake of mobility is worthwhile.

Electrical connections

By the time you have bought a synth, a few expanders, a sequencer, an effects unit, a small mixer, amplifier and the various other items that go to make up a studio, you will probably find that you have 20 or so plugs to fit into, perhaps, a couple of mains sockets. The most obvious thing to do is to buy a few four-way mains blocks, some two and three way mains adaptors and just cobble the whole lot together into ... a potential disaster.

There are two points to look at, namely the safety of your connections and the current draw of the pieces of equipment.

If possible, you should consider running a separate power supply from the fuse box to your studio and terminate it with an isolating switch. The advantage of the separate supply is the lack of mains borne noises such as clicks from refrigerators and other pieces of equipment turning on and off. The isolating switch allows you to cut all electricity in case of an emergency. If you cannot entertain this idea, then it is worth considering building some small boards with mains blocks attached to them, each with a switch to allow you to disconnect that board from the mains.

Make sure you use good quality plugs that have a plastic sleeve on the positive and neutral pins, and that you also use good quality mains blocks and adaptors (if you have to). While it may be difficult to overload the fuse in a block, it is easy for a plug or adaptor to pull half out - it is better to use a few extra blocks and to avoid adaptors completely. Remember to label each plug with the name of the piece of equipment it is attached to!

It is highly unlikely that the total current being drawn by your equipment is anywhere near the standard 13 amps that is allowed for by the fuse in the plug connected to your mains socket. Working out the total current draw of your system is quite simple; there is a plate on the rear of most MIDI products which has the serial number and the power required for that unit, in Watts. Add up all the power figures for your system and divide by 240. This will give you the total current drawn by your system. While you may find that a 16-track tape recorder requires a couple of amps, synths and the like usually draw less than a tenth of an amp. Consequently, your entire system will probably have a current draw of less than 5 amps.

Work out the current draw for each piece of equipment, get hold of a selection of low-value fuses (1, 2 and 3 amps) and substitute these for the standard 13 amp variety that comes as standard with a UK mains plug. This will then ensure that should a fault occur with a piece of equipment drawing, say, a quarter of an amp, the fuse in its plug will blow first. Any mains blocks you are using should have 13 amp fuses in so that you don't need to worry about the total current draw for all the equipment connected to this block.

When you turn on some pieces of equipment, the initial surge may draw more current than under normal running conditions. If you leave all your equipment on and then turn on at the wall, the instantaneous current draw could exceed 13 amps and blow fuses. Other damage is also possible when current surges occur. For safety sake, many people prefer to turn each individual piece of equipment on and off.

Time for a hum!

One of the most common problems is a low frequency hum coming from the loudspeakers. This is usually due to trouble with earthing in one or more pieces of equipment and is called an earth loop (Figure 8.1). As mentioned in Chapter 3, it is impossible for a correctly wired MIDI cable, which is connected to a MIDI device adhering to the rules of MIDI, to cause an earth loop. However, MIDI equipment also has mains and audio leads (Figure 8-1). This creates a simple transformer which picks up mains interference and appears as hum in the audio signal.

If a common point for the audio lead screen and mains earth exists inside the synth, an earth loop is created. The easiest way to break the loop is to remove the earth lead inside the synth's mains plug. Unfortunately, this is also the most dangerous way as you are relying on the audio connection to provide the earth for the synth. Should a fault occur within the synth and the audio leads not be connected, you stand a very real chance of an electric shock. The correct way to break the loop is to ensure that the audio system is earthed and to have a 3300 ohm resistor wired in line with the screen in the offending item's jack plug (Figure 8-2).

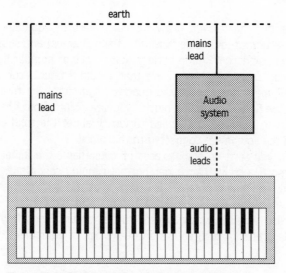

Figure 8-1 The makings of an earth loop

The situation outside of the UK, in the USA for instance, is that most MIDI equipment is connected to the mains by a two-core cable which lacks an earth. If this is the case, there is less likelihood of an earth loop. The basic rule is that if a piece of equipment requires an earth connection to the mains, make sure that this connection is made.

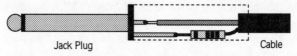

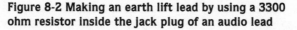

Jack Plug   Cable

Figure 8-2 Making an earth lift lead by using a 3300 ohm resistor inside the jack plug of an audio lead

If you have, say, three MIDI devices in a rack with only one turned on and you can hear earth hum, don't immediately jump to the conclusion that this must be the problem piece of equipment. A piece of equipment can cause an earth loop even if it is turned off as the mains and audio connections are still being made. If there are earth loop problems with racked equipment, remove the mains plug for each item and start racking them again one at a time.

Sometimes, hum can be heard even though an earth loop is not the cause. A common example is when pieces of equipment are very close together, a situation that commonly occurs in a rack system and is called 'proximity hum'. The electrical field from a mains transformer may interfere with the operation of another piece of equipment and exhibit itself as hum. Another common situation is with mains adaptors built into plugs where the electrical field is picked up by other mains leads close by.

Two final points. Try not to run audio, mains and MIDI cables next to each other. While there are unlikely to be problems with good quality audio and MIDI cables, it is quite easy for the mains leads to induce hum if the cable quality is poor. If you have to run such cables near to each other, make them cross at right angles to minimise hum problems. Also, beware of computer monitors; audio leads run anywhere near one of these invariably picks up hum from the radiated electrical field.

9

What is my MIDI equipment capable of?

If all else fails...

...read the manual! If only life was that simple with MIDI! Anyone who has bought MIDI equipment will be aware of the possible pitfalls when trying to work out whether what you are buying is what you think you are buying. A twenty minute demonstration in a shop is unlikely to turn up those annoying failings of a piece of equipment that you intend to use for a couple of years. The main problem area is in matching a synth to a sound module. What MIDI information can the synth send out? Can the sound module respond to it? How does your effects unit use MIDI program changes?

The obvious thing is to read the information at the beginning of the manual where the features and facilities are explained. You could think of a few things you want to check and look them up in the manual, but manuals are generally unfriendly beasts. However, there is one part of the manual that is pretty clear in what it tells you, and it happens to be hidden away right at the back of the manual.

MIDI implementation charts

A MIDI implementation chart (abbreviated to MI chart from here onwards) attempts to indicate how a MIDI device will behave in all situations. The easiest way to follow this chapter is to have an MI chart for a synth in front of you and to check the various parts as the chapter progresses. If you do not have one to hand, Figure 9-1 is a typical synth chart while Figure 9-2 is a chart for a typical sound module. Not all functions will be looked at; any that are rarely used will be ignored.

MODEL Synthesiser   MIDI Implementation Chart

Function...		Transmitted	Recognised	Remarks
Basic	Default	1-16	1-16	Memorised
Channel	Change	1-16	1-16	
	Default	3	1, 2, 3, 4	Memorised
Mode	Messages	MONO, POLY	MONO, POLY	
	Altered	****************	X	
Note		28 - 103	0 - 127	
Number	True Voice	****************	0 - 127	
Velocity	Note ON	O 9nH, v=1-127	O v=1-127	
	Note OFF	X 9nH, v=0	X	
After	Key's	X	X	
Touch	Ch's	O	O	
Pitch Bender		O	O	9 bit resolution
	0, 32	O	*1	Bank select
	1	O	O	Modulation
	7	O	O	Volume
Control	10	O	O	Pan
	11	O	O	Expression
	64	O	*1	Sustain pedal
Change	65	O	*1	Portamento
	121	O	O	Reset all controllers
Prog		O 0-63	O 0-63	
Change	True #	****************	*2	
System Exclusive		O	O	Voices
System	: Song Pos	X	X	
	: Song Sel	X	X	
Common	: Tune	X	X	
System	: Clock	X	X	
Real Time	: Commands	X	X	
Aux	: Local ON/OFF	X	O	
Mes-	: All Notes Off	O	O	
sages	: Active Sense	O	O	
	: Reset	X	X	

Notes   *1 OX selectable
         *2 bank 1: 0-31, bank 2: 32-63

Mode 1 : OMNI ON, POLY   Mode 2 : OMNI ON, MONO   O : Yes
Mode 3 : OMNI OFF, POLY   Mode 4 : OMNI OFF, MONO   X : No

Figure 9-1 MIDI implementation chart for a typical synthesiser

MODEL Sound Module   MIDI Implementation Chart

Function...		Transmitted	Recognised	Remarks
Basic	Default	X	1 - 16	Memorised
Channel	Change	X	1 - 16	
Mode	Default	X	1, 2, 3, 4	Memorised
	Messages	X	X	
	Altered	*****************	X	
Note		X	0 - 127	
Number	True Voice	*****************	1 - 127	
Velocity	Note ON	X	O v=1-127	
	Note OFF	X	X	
After	Key's	X	X	
Touch	Ch's	X	O	
Pitch Bender		X	O 0-12 semi	9 bit resolution
	1	X	O	Modulation
	5	X	O	Portamento time
	7	X	O	Volume
Control	10	X	O	Pan
	11	X	O	Expression
	64	X	O	Sustain pedal
Change	65	X	O	Portamento
	67	X	O	Soft pedal
	121	X	O	Reset all controllers
Prog		X	*1	
Change	True #	*****************	0-127	
System Exclusive		O	O	
System	: Song Pos	X	X	
	: Song Sel	X	X	
Common	: Tune	X	X	
System	: Clock	X	X	
Real Time	: Commands	X	X	
Aux	: Local ON/OFF	X	X	
Mes-	: All Notes Off	X	O	
sages	: Active Sense	X	O	
	: Reset	X	X	
Notes	*1 OX selectable			

Mode 1 : OMNI ON, POLY   Mode 2 : OMNI ON, MONO   O : Yes
Mode 3 : OMNI OFF, POLY   Mode 4 : OMNI OFF, MONO   X : No

Figure 9-2 MIDI implementation chart for a typical sound module

All charts should have the following:
- Model name, date and version at the top of the page.
- Four columns labelled Function, Transmitted, Recognised and Remarks respectively.
- Information on Modes 1 to 4 at the foot of the chart.
- A key to the symbols used in the chart - generally 'O' is Yes and 'X' is No.

'Function' lists all the various MIDI messages that are used by MIDI devices while 'Transmitted' and 'Recognised' show exactly what can be sent out from the MIDI Out port and recognised at the MIDI In port. A comment in the 'Remarks' column usually helps to clarify how the function being looked at works.

At the bottom of the table is a Notes section. This can enlarge on any detail for which there is insufficient space elsewhere in the chart.

Channels and modes

Basic channel shows what MIDI channels the device can use with Default being the one that is set when the device is first turned on. If the comment 'memorised' appears in the Remark then the device has a battery-backed memory which remembers the MIDI channels you set the unit to transmit and receive on when you turn it off.

Four modes exist in MIDI, and these are quickly itemised at the foot of the table. Omni On means that the device will respond to MIDI information on any MIDI channel, a situation that is rarely (if ever) called for and as Modes 1 and 2 both use Omni On, they are hardly ever used. Mode 3 (Omni Off, Poly) means that a single MIDI channel is used for sending or receiving many notes. A typical example would be playing a four-note chord on a synth; the notes are all transmitted on one MIDI channel. Mode 4 is mainly used on guitar synths which require a different MIDI channel per string.

The idea of a true multi-timbral synth capable of playing many notes on each of various MIDI channels did not exist when the MI chart was constructed. Consequently, modes are generally irrelevant where today's MIDI instruments are concerned.

Notes

The full range of MIDI notes stretches to over ten and a half octaves, from MIDI Note #0 to MIDI Note #127. Each note can also be written as a combination of a letter and number, the letter being the standard one for the note while the number shows the octave. Middle C on a keyboard is MIDI Note #60 and is usually referred to as C4. Consequently, C3 is an octave lower and C5 an octave higher.

Transmitted Note Number shows the range of MIDI Note numbers that a synth can send out. Isn't this simply the number of notes on the keyboard? Not necessarily, as the synth may have a transpose facility and this is included. Recognised Note Number shows the range of notes that the sound module will respond to. What happens if a note is received outside of the range of notes that the synth can actually play? True Voice shows how such notes are handled. The usual method is to transpose such notes up or down as necessary until the note falls within the synth's capabilities.

Is the synth keyboard velocity sensitive? Check the Velocity part of the MI chart. If the Transmitted column has an 'O' next to the Note On function, then the answer is yes. An 'X' means the answer is no.

Aftertouch and pitch bend

Aftertouch is the ability of a keyboard to send additional MIDI information, after a key has been initially played, by an increase in pressure on the key. How this information is used is down to the attached sound module, but the bringing in of vibrato or pitch change of the notes are two common results.

There are two types of aftertouch. Channel pressure uses an average value for all the fingers currently pressing down on keys while Key pressure allows each finger to have a different value. The former is by far the more common. If you have an MI chart for a sound module, check the Recognised column. If this has an 'X', then whether or not a synth transmits Aftertouch is irrelevant as this sound module cannot respond to it.

An 'O' in the Transmit pitch bender column means that the synth has a pitch bend wheel. The Remarks column will probably have a comment about the resolution being so-many bits. Suffice to say that the higher the number, the smoother the possible change of pitch via the pitch bend wheel.

Control changes

This is probably the most important section in the chart. MIDI control changes are generally used to alter the performance of a sound module and are often called MIDI controllers. This can be confusing as a MIDI controller is also any device that can transmit MIDI information!

The transmitted column tells you which control changes your synth can send out MIDI information for, the most common ones being #1 (Modulation), #7 (Volume), #10 (Pan) and #64 (Sustain Pedal). However, this must be matched up with the same control changes in the Recognise column of your sound module. For instance, if your synth has an 'O' next to control change #7 (Volume) in the Transmitted column, this means that moving its volume fader sends out MIDI Volume information. If your sound module has an 'X' next to this function, or no mention of it at all, then it will not respond to this. Moving the volume fader on the synth will have no effect on the volume level of the sound module.

Also check whether your synth Transmits and Recognises the same control changes. MIDI Volume is a typical one which some synths will respond to but do not transmit when their volume faders are moved.

Changing patches

A collection of settings held in a MIDI device's memory is generally called a Patch, the word being a hangover from the days when synth players plugged patch leads into various sockets on a synth to set up a particular sound. Most synths, sound modules and effects units have many patches in memory, each of which calls up a different sound or effect. Using MIDI program changes allows you to remotely access these.

There are two different approaches to patch changing. The first is simply to send a program change number between 0 and 127 from, say, the buttons on a synth. For instance, if a sound module you are using has an Electric Piano as patch number 5 on MIDI channel 4,

73

set the synth to transmit on MIDI channel 4 and press the button that will select patch number 5. If a sound module has more than 128 patches, this procedure will generally not work. The alternative is to set up a 'Program Table'. on the receiving device. This assigns a particular internal patch to an incoming MIDI program change number. For example, the sound module may receive MIDI program change number 15 and call up patch 138. This method is very common with effects units.

The MI chart shows the range of program changes that can be Transmitted while a different range of values in the Recognised column usually means that a program table is being used.

System information

Aftertouch, pitch bend and control changes are all performance-type functions that are used to make playing synths and sound modules more interesting. Some functions are required purely to make the set-up run smoothly. The next three sections in the chart deal with such System functions.

System exclusive

System exclusive is generally used to transfer sound settings between synths and librarians for storage purposes. SysEx, for short, is so named because each manufacturer has a MIDI ID code and individual codes for each piece of equipment. An 'O' here normally means that you can record the internal memory to a sequencer track and get them back by replaying that track once you have experimented and lost the original settings!

System common

System common are functions aimed at every MIDI device in a system, irrespective of which MIDI channel they are set to receive on. The useful one here is Song Pos, short for Song Position Pointer mentioned in Chapter 6. Check whether there is an 'O' in the Recognise column of your drum machine; if not, a song will always start from the beginning no matter where your sequencer commences play-back from. This is if your sequencer can send out Song Position Pointers; check the Transmit column in the MI chart for an 'O'.

System real time

System real time functions are all to do with timing information. Clock is short for MIDI Clock, the basic timing message, while Commands refers to Start, Stop and Continue. A good MI chart will list which of these are valid; a bad one will just have an 'O' which does not necessarily mean that all three are catered for.

Auxiliary messages

Four final functions are grouped together under this heading. Of these, the most important is Local ON/OFF which shows whether you can split the keyboard from its sounds in a synth as mentioned in Chapter 4. Even if an 'X' is shown here, the synth may have a non-standard method of providing Local control Off such as assigning control of the sounds to MIDI. Such a facility will not show up on an MI chart. Also, some synths do not have a Local Control Off switch on-board but will respond to a Local Off MIDI message. If there is no mention of Local Off for your synth but an 'O' exists in the Recognise column, see if your sequencer can transmit the relevant message.

General check

Synth

If you are buying a synth it is worth checking the MI chart, especially the following areas of the Transmitted column:

- Basic channel; is it 1-16? If not, the synth can only transmit on a specific MIDI channel.
- Velocity Note ON; is the velocity range 1-127 or 64? The latter means that the keyboard is not velocity sensitive so hitting the keys with a feather or sledge-hammer will have no effect on the level of the sounds from your expander.
- Aftertouch; is there an 'O' in the Channel column? If not, the keyboard is not pressure sensitive and any features on your sound module that require aftertouch will be useless.
- Control changes; does the synth transmit the basic ones - Modulation, Volume, Pan and Sustain Pedal? Do they match up with the list for your sound module?

- Program changes; can the synth transmit these? Very useful for remotely selecting patches on sound modules.
- Auxiliary Messages; Does the synth support Local Off?

Sound module

If you are buying a sound module, check the following in the Recognised column:

- Basic Channel; is it 1-16? If not, the module can only respond to MIDI information on certain MIDI channels.
- Velocity Note On; is there an 'O' here? If not, the level of sound cannot be controlled by how hard you play the keys on the synth.
- Aftertouch; Is there an 'O' here for Channels? If not, there are no functions in the sound module that can be controlled via aftertouch.
- Control changes; does the module recognise the basic ones - Modulation, Volume, Pan and Sustain Pedal? Do they match up with the list for your synth?
- Program changes; can the module recognise these? If so, you can select patches via a program change facility on your synth.

General MIDI

Horses for courses

MIDI is MIDI, right? Not quite. While the whole idea of MIDI is compatibility between products from different manufacturers, there are many areas that are left open to the manufacturer, including:

- Program change numbers and which instruments they select.
- Percussion sounds and which MIDI Note numbers they are assigned to.
- How many simultaneous notes a sound module can play (the polyphony).
- The MIDI control changes that a MIDI device transmits or responds to.

What happens if someone brings a song file to play back on your MIDI system. For the moment, let's assume that you are both using the same sequencer so that you can load up the song and start playing it. Are you likely to hear the same result as the person who originally recorded the song? Probably not. Have a look at the following problems and then see why General MIDI offers a possible solution.

Wrong program changes

Let's say that track 1 of the song is intended to be piano on MIDI channel 2. There are three possible results:

- You have a sound module set to a piano sound on MIDI channel 2. Result; piano plays.
- You have a sound module set to a different sound on MIDI channel 2. Result; wrong sound.

• No sound module is set to receive on MIDI channel 2. Result; no sound at all.

If the original composer has placed a MIDI Program change message at the beginning of the track, the situation will be even worse if you are using a different sound module. The first situation above, where you correctly had a piano sound set for MIDI channel 2, will now have a different sound called up.

Wrong drum mapping

Now that the instruments have been sorted, what about the percussion side? Well, the drums for this song are on various tracks, each assigned to MIDI channel 5. Each drum is played by a particular MIDI Note number, with the group of numbers being called the 'drum mapping'. Again, there are three possible results:

• You have drum sounds on MIDI channel 5 with the same drum mapping. Result; drums play.
• You have drum sounds on MIDI channel 5 with a different drum mapping. Result; the wrong drums play.
• MIDI channel 5 is assigned to a different instrument. Result; the drum rhythm is played on the wrong instrument!

If the drum mapping is different, you will have to change the MIDI note numbers for every percussion instrument. While you can partly do this via the transpose function of the sequencer, this is of little use if you have, say, four toms and a couple of crashes on the same track. Individually changing their note numbers is a long and laborious job.

Not enough polyphony

Instruments and drums sorted, can we play the song satisfactorily now? Let's say that when the composer recorded the original song, two expanders and a drum machine were used, the latter purely as a sound module. Each of these can play, say, 8 notes and the drum machine can handle a kit of 8 drums. That makes a total polyphony of 24 notes.

You, on the other hand, have a single multi-timbral sound module with a polyphony of 12 notes. What happens when one instrument is sustaining a five-note chord and the sustain pedal is being used heavily on the piano? The drums cut out because the 12-note polyphony limit of your expander has been reached!

Lacking in performance

Using MIDI control changes sensibly can add immeasurably to the performance of a song. Modulation (#1) can be used to add that extra touch of vibrato, while MIDI Volume (#7) can control the dynamics of a song and also be used for fades in and out. That is if the sound

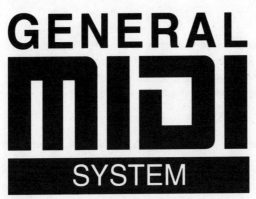

Figure 10-1 The official General MIDI logo

module you are playing the song through is capable of responding to the particular control changes...

Picture the scene where, having worked out all the other problems, you play the song through on your system and at the end where the fade out has been programmed, nothing happens!

General MIDI system

Due in no small part to the above situations, a class of MIDI sound module has been created, essentially for the consumer market. Any sound module or synth bearing the General MIDI logo (Figure 10-1) guarantees the following:

- Ability to play up to 16 instruments (timbres) on any MIDI channels. All GM modules are effectively 16 part multi-timbral.
- Key-based drums on MIDI channel 10 and following the General MIDI Percussion Map (Figure10-2).
- A minimum of 24 simultaneously-available voices, possibly with 8 reserved for percussion and 16 for other instruments.
- •128 presets each assigned to the correct MIDI program change number in the General MIDI Sound Set (Figure 10-3).
- Recognition of the following MIDI control changes; Modulation (#1), Volume (#7), Pan (#10), Expression (#11) and Sustain Pedal (#64).
- Recognition of channel aftertouch and pitch bend.

Given the above, a high degree of compatibility should be exhibited by any synth with the GM logo and the main idea is one of simplicity. The standard MIDI sockets, a stereo pair of audio outputs, a headphones socket and a master volume control are all that a GM sound module needs.

#	Drum sound	#	Drum sound	#	Drum sound
35	Acoustic Bass Drum	51	Ride Cymbal 1	67	High Agogo
36	Bass Drum 1	52	Chinese Cymbal	68	Low Agogo
37	Side Stick	53	Ride Bell	69	Cabasa
38	Acoustic Snare	54	Tambourine	70	Maracas
39	Hand Clap	55	Splash Cymbal	71	Short Whistle
40	Electric Snare	56	Cowbell	72	Long Whistle
41	Low Floor Tom	57	Crash Cymbal 2	73	Short Guiro
42	Closed Hi-Hat	58	Vibraslap	74	Long Guiro
43	High Floor Tom	59	Ride Cymbal 2	75	Claves
44	Pedal Hi-Hat	60	Hi Bongo	76	Hi Wood Block
45	Low Tom	61	Low Bongo	77	Low Wood Block
46	Open Hi-Hat	62	Mute Hi Conga	78	Mute Cuica
47	Low Mid Tom	63	Open Hi conga	79	Open Cuica
48	Hi Mid Tom	64	Low Conga	80	Mute Triangle
49	Crash Cymbal 1	65	High Timbale	81	Open Triangle
50	High Tom	66	Low Timbale		

Figure 10.2 The General MIDI percussion map

Working with General MIDI

The main problem that you are likely to get when recording a song on a sequencer with a single GM sound module is that of 'voice stealing'. When you exceed the 24 available voices, notes start to cut out. If you think of the 24 voices as counters living in a box, the secret is to try to return them to the box as quickly as possible after being used. Here are eight useful guidelines:

- Reduce all notes for percussion sounds to the shortest possible length. A drum sound triggers as soon as it receives a MIDI Note On so the shorter the length of the note, the quicker the voice can be ready for re-using.

- Some sounds require two voices to build that sound. For instance, Pad 1 (New Age) might use a breathy sound overlaid with a bell-like sound. Use as few two-voice sounds as possible because they halve the available polyphony.

- Use the sustain pedal with great care. Take the example of a piano. Playing a five-note chord, hitting the sustain pedal and following up with a five-note melody ties up a total of 10 voices. If you fail to release the sustain pedal before you play the next chord, a total of 15 voices will be in use. This is likely to cut out other instruments playing on the beat of the bar, the most crowded point.

- Simplify your chords. There is little point in playing a five-note piano or pad chord that is intended to be in the background when two of the notes are being duplicated by other instruments.

- Once the polyphony is exceeded, most GM sound modules will give priority to MIDI channel 10 followed by 1, 2, 3 and so on up to 16. Record the important instruments on the lower-numbered MIDI channels so that if note-stealing occurs you are less likely to hear it happening.

- Take care when using the quantise function on a sequencer. This auto-corrects timing mistakes in your playing and will, for example, place all notes intended for the first beat of the bar on the first beat of the bar. Lots of notes at one place in a song are likely to lead to note-stealing and manually moving a few notes slightly may get around this.

81

- If you are not going to be able to hear a particular note, don't record it! For instance, there is little point in having a hihat playing at the same time as a strong snare drum because it will be masked by the snare sound.
- Thin out non-note data where possible by using the relevant function on the sequencer. Aftertouch and pitch bend information can often be reduced to half of the original amount without any audible difference.

#	Instrument	#	Instrument	#	Instrument	#	Instrument
1	Acoustic Grand Piano	33	Acoustic Bass	65	Soprano Sax	97	FX 1 (rain)
2	Bright Acoustic Piano	34	Electric Bass (finger)	66	Alto Sax	98	FX 2 (soundtrack)
3	Electric Grand Piano	35	Electric Bass (pick)	67	Tenor Sax	99	FX 3 (crystal)
4	Honky-tonk Piano	36	Fretless Bass	68	Baritone Sax	100	FX 4 (atmosphere)
5	Electric Piano 1	37	Slap Bass	69	Oboe	101	FX 5 (brightness)
6	Electric Piano 2	38	Slap Bass 2	70	English Horn	102	FX 6 (goblins)
7	Harpsichord	39	Synth Bass 1	71	Bassoon	103	FX 7 (echoes)
8	Clavi	40	Synth Bass 2	72	Clarinet	104	FX 8 (sci-fi)
9	Celesta	41	Violin	73	Piccolo	105	Sitar
10	Glockenspiel	42	Viola	74	Flute	106	Banjo
11	Music Box	43	Cello	75	Recorder	107	Shamisen
12	Vibraphone	44	Contrabass	76	Pan Flute	108	Koto
13	Marimba	45	Tremolo Strings	77	Blown Bottle	109	Kalimba
14	Xylophone	46	Pizzicato Strings	78	Shakuhachi	110	Bagpipe
15	Tubular Bells	47	Orchestral Harp	79	Whistle	111	Fiddle
16	Dulcimer	48	Timpani	80	Ocarina	112	Shanai
17	Drawbar Organ	49	String Ensemble 1	81	Lead 1 (square)	113	Tinkle Bell
18	Percussive Organ	50	String Ensemble 2	82	Lead 2 (sawtooth)	114	Agogo
19	Rock Organ	51	SynthStrings 1	83	Lead 3 (calliope	115	Steel Drums
20	Church Organ	52	SynthStrings 2	84	Lead 4 (chiff)	116	Woodblock
21	Reed Organ	53	Choir Aahs	85	Lead 5 (charang)	117	Taiko Drum
22	Accordion	54	Voice Oohs	86	Lead 6 (voice)	118	Melodic Tom
23	Harmonica	55	Synth Voice	87	Lead 7 (fifths)	119	Synth Drum
24	Tango Accordion	56	Orchestra Hit	88	Lead 8 (bass + lead)	120	Reverse Cymbal
25	Acoustic Guitar (nylon)	57	Trumpet	89	Pad 1 (new age)	121	Guitar Fret Noise
26	Acoustic Guitar (steel)	58	Trombone	90	Pad 2 (warm)	122	Breath Noise
27	Electric Guitar (jazz)	59	Tuba	91	Pad 3 (polysynth)	123	Seashore
28	Electric Guitar (clean)	60	Muted Trumpet	92	Pad 4 (choir)	124	Bird Tweet
29	Electric Guitar (muted)	61	French Horn	93	Pad 5 (bowed)	125	Telephone Ring
30	Overdriven Guitar	62	Brass Section	94	Pad 6 (metallic)	126	Helicopter
31	Distortion Guitar	63	SynthBrass 1	95	Pad 7 (halo)	127	Applause
32	Guitar Harmonics	64	SynthBrass 2	96	Pad 8 (sweep)	128	Gunshot

Figure 10-3 The General MIDI Sound Set

11

Moving songs between different sequencers

Using MIDI files

While sequencing programs on a computer use a disk drive to save their data to a disk, you cannot take a song recorded on one sequencer and simply load it into a different one - the way in which the data is stored on disk is not the same.

In 1987, various software companies decided that a common file format for the saving of songs on a sequencer was required. The Standard MIDI File Specification was the result of this and is used by almost every sequencer writer, irrespective of the computer or sequencing program. This has led to a high degree of compatibility in the transfer of songs.

There are three types of MIDI File:
- Format 0 saves the entire song as a single track.
- Format 1 keeps sequencer tracks separate within a song.
- Format 2 saves a song as a series of patterns.

The most commonly used type is Format 1, especially as there is almost no limitation to the number of tracks that can be saved (unless you call around 64,000 a restriction!). Most computer-based sequencers give you the option of saving a song in either their own format or as a MIDI File, the latter usually being referred to as 'exporting' the song and 'importing' it on loading.

On loading a MIDI File, you will notice at least one, and possibly two, irregularities. Any MIDI channel numbers that were associated with each sequencer track will have disappeared, and it is quite possible that the track names will have also vanished. The latter is because there are two ways of saving track names in a MIDI File and depending on the methods used by the sequencer you recorded the song on and the sequencer you are now loading it into, the names may or may not still be there. The tracks will, of course, still be in the same order.

The point about the MIDI channel assignments disappearing is an important one. If you recall, rechanneling (see page 26) is something that you do to affect the play-back of a track, to ensure that the notes and other MIDI information are received by the correct sound module. Information used solely for play-back purposes is not usually saved in a MIDI File. If your sequencer allows you to use play-back track delays, transposing and so on, check for the function that allows this information to be saved with the MIDI File.

Instead of using a sequencer for live performances, you may decide to get a MIDI File player. This simply plays back MIDI Files from a disk without allowing you to carry out any editing, but has the very real advantage of playing straight from the disk and so eliminates any waiting between songs. If you intend to use one of these, check which MIDI File format it uses. If it is Format 0, then you will have to save your MIDI Files in this format on the sequencer. Many sequencers do not give you the option; if the song is made up of a single track, it saves it as Format 0 otherwise it uses Format 1. To force it to save in Format 0, merge all the tracks down to a single track and then save as a MIDI File.

MIDI Files can even be transferred between different computers although a stage of conversion may be necessary depending on whether the second computer can read disks from the first.

Using sequencer to sequencer connections

So what happens if your sequencer cannot work with MIDI Files, which is true for most dedicated units? Why might you want to transfer songs from such a unit?

• You may have bought a new sequencer!
• Your current sequencer might have no disk drive and yet you want to safeguard some of your important songs.
• You might use a computer-based sequencer in the studio but a dedicated sequencer live.

Whatever the reason, surely transferring songs is simply a matter of connecting the MIDI Out of the first sequencer to the MIDI In of the second and just playing a song on the first and recording it on the second? Not quite. There are a few problems that need to be overcome if the song transfer is to be successful:

- The two sequencers must keep in time with each other.
- The transference must not damage the timing of the song information.

The second point is very important. There is little use in spending days carefully recording and editing your song if, after transfer, it sounds rather different. Let's take the situation of transferring songs from a dedicated sequencer to a computer-based one (Figure 11-1) and use the terms sequencer and computer to describe the two devices.

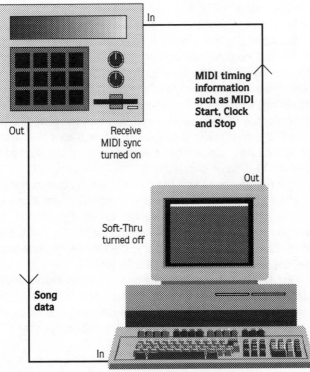

Figure 11-1 Transferring songs from a dedicated sequencer to a computer-based one

The set-up is as follows:
- Connect the MIDI Out from the sequencer to the MIDI In of the computer. All MIDI song information will pass along this cable.
- Connect the MIDI Out from the computer to the MIDI In of the sequencer. MIDI timing information will travel down this cable to keep the two devices in time with each other.
- Set the sequencer to receive MIDI sync, commonly called 'External Sync' mode.
- Turn soft-Thru off on the computer, otherwise the song data received at the MIDI In will be merged with its MIDI sync messages and retransmitted from the MIDI Out. This will affect the regularity of the MIDI Clock messages and hence the timing of the transfer.
- Set the computer to record. It will send out the necessary MIDI Start and Clock messages to keep the sequencer in time.

The second point of not damaging the timing of the song information is more difficult to ensure. If all tracks on the sequencer have been quantised, slow the tempo of the computer down to 60 beats per minute (BPM), turn all the sequencer tracks on, record on the computer and requantise. If on play-back you find that the song has not quantised correctly, re-transfer it but either a few tracks at a time or at a slower tempo. Any unquantised tracks should be transferred on their own and at 60 BPM or slower.

The reason the tempo has to be slowed is due to the nature of MIDI. While lots of MIDI information wants to travel along the MIDI cable, only one message at a time can do so. By slowing down the transfer you stand more chance of keeping the integrity of the timing. It all comes down to timing vs accuracy; the more accurately you wish to transfer the songs, the longer it will take you!

One final point. Can your sequencer unmix tracks according to their MIDI channel? If not, and you intend to carry out some editing on the computer, you will have to transfer the song one track at a time, recording each track on a separate track of the computer.

What happens If ...

... something goes wrong. The nature of MIDI makes this very possible, but most problems can be sorted out by logically considering the situation.

General problems

You turn on a device and it doesn't work;
• Make sure that the mains lead is plugged in at the back of the unit.
• Check the fuse at the wall (or fuse box) by plugging in something that you know is working - a light possibly.
• Change the fuse in the plug.

Synth problems

You press keys and there is no sound;
• Check that the audio side is turned on and that the volume is not set to zero.
• Check the audio connections - remember, sound doesn't travel down a MIDI cable.
• Make sure that Local Control is turned on.

Problems with a synth and connected sound module(s)

You press keys and there is no sound;

- Check the MIDI connections - the MIDI Out from the synth should be plugged into the MIDI In of the sound module.
- Check that the audio side is correctly connected. If the synth has a 'demo song' facility, try it.
- Are you using a MIDI daisy chain connection? If so, check that all devices between the synth and sound module are turned on - a MIDI Thru will not operate unless the MIDI device is turned on.
- Check that the MIDI transmit channel for the synth is the same as the MIDI receive channel for the sound module. Try setting the MIDI receive of the sound module to Omni On.
- Is there a volume pedal attached? If so, press it flat down which should be the position for fully on.
- Did you press keys before turning on the sound module? If so, the sound module may have missed some vital MIDI information. Twiddle the pitch bend wheel and press the keys again or else turn the synth off and then back on.

Notes are hanging on after you stop playing;

- Have you changed MIDI channel while holding down some notes? If so, MIDI Notes Off have been lost. Try playing the same notes again, which sometimes works, or turn the sound module off and then back on.
- Has a MIDI cable been accidentally disconnected?

The wrong sound is playing;

- If the sound module is multi-timbral, are you playing the correct part?
- Have you accidentally sent a MIDI Program Change message?

Sequencer problems

You press keys on a connected keyboard and there is no sound from your sound module;
- Check that MIDI notes are being sent from the synth - connect it directly to the sound module as a test.
- Check the MIDI receive channel for the sound module and make certain that the current sequencer track has been rechanneled to the same MIDI channel number.
- Is the sequencer's soft-Thru turned on?
- Is the MIDI cable faulty? Try a different one.

The synth is sending certain MIDI messages but the sound module isn't responding to them;
- Check whether any of the sequencer's input or output filters are turned on.

Notes are unexpectedly cutting off;
- Are you exceeding the sound module's polyphony? If so, voice-stealing is taking place.
- Are All Notes Off messages being recorded on the sequencer? Set the sequencer's input filter to prevent this.

The polyphony of the synth appears to be halved and there is a slight delay from sounds;
- Turn Local Control Off on the keyboard. Two voices are being played by each key press, one due to the key and the other due to the information being received at the MIDI In socket from the sequencer. If your synth doesn't have Local Control, see whether the sequencer has a 'MIDI off channel' that prevents this duplication.

The sound is out of tune;
- Is the transpose feature of the sequencer active? Set it to '0'.
- Did you stop recording while the pitch bend wheel was away from the central position? Re-centre it.

- Did you stop the sequencer in the middle of a section of pitch bend information? If the sequencer has a 'Chase' function, activate it.

The sequencer doesn't appear to have as much memory as it should;
- Filter out any unwanted messages. If you're recording drums, make sure that the transmission of Aftertouch is turned off on the keyboard.
- If your sequencer allows you to, thin out MIDI information such as Pitch Bend, Aftertouch and MIDI Control Changes.

There is no sound on play-back;
- Is the sequencer track muted? Unmute it!
- Have you correctly set the MIDI channels?

The sounds on play-back are different to the ones you had when you recorded;
- Have you changed sound module? Remember that MIDI only records note and performance information, not the actual sounds.
- Have you recorded any MIDI Program Changes? If you are using a different sound module now, the sounds are likely to be on different Program Change numbers.

Notes are hanging on after the sequencer has stopped playing;
- Check that a MIDI cable hasn't been accidentally disconnected.
- Notes Off have been lost, possibly through editing the position of notes. Check this on an Event list.

Drum machine problems

The drum machine won't sync with the sequencer;
- Does the drum machine have this ability? Not all do; check the System Real Time section of the MIDI Implementation chart

which should have an 'O' in the Recognised column of both the Clock and Commands functions.

- Check the MIDI connections. The MIDI Out from the sequencer should be connected to the MIDI In of the drum machine, although possibly via a MIDI daisy chain arrangement.
- Make sure that the sequencer's MIDI Sync Transmit is turned on and that the drum machine is set to receive MIDI sync.
- You may need to press 'Play' on your drum machine to put it into a 'Ready' mode to receive MIDI Sync information.

The drum machine and sequencer are in sync but the drum machine is playing odd notes as well;
- Turn off the drum machine's Note Receive function.
- If this is impossible, set the drum machine to a MIDI channel that is not being used by the sequencer and make certain that Omni Off is selected.

Using the drum machine as a sound module, no sounds appear;
- Check that MIDI Note receive is set on the drum machine.
- Check that the MIDI receive channel for the drum machine is the same as the MIDI transmit channel of the drum track on the sequencer.

Multi-track problems

Your sequencer won't sync with your multi-track recorder;
- Have you recorded tape sync or time code onto tape?
- Is the level correct? Check the manual.
- Is the signal on an adjacent track interfering? Try a new tape and see whether the problem persists.
- Check the MIDI connections. The MIDI Out from the tape sync converter should be linked to the MIDI In of the sequencer.
- Check the audio connections. The Audio Out from the multi-track should be connected to the Audio In of the tape sync converter.

- Is your sequencer set to receive MIDI sync or MIDI Time Code, depending on the type of tape sync converter? Have you made the correct choice?

Your sequencer always plays from the beginning of the song;

- Does your sequencer recognise Song Position Pointers? If not, it will always commence from the beginning of a song.

Your sequencer stops for no apparent reason in the middle of a song while playing in sync;

- Have you recorded enough code on tape?
- If it is a temporary pause, it is likely to be tape damage. Listen to the tape code and see if you can hear any alteration to the tone. If so, re-record the code for the particular song on a different track although it may be very difficult to successfully re-sync the code with the song.
- If it is a total stop, try turning the sequencer off and then back on.

Your sequencer goes out of sync with the multi-track;

- If it is at the beginning of the song and you are using SMPTE time code, check that you have selected the correct frame rate on the sequencer.
- If it is in the middle of the song and you are using SMPTE time code, check that any tempo or time signature changes have been entered into the tape sync converter.
- Is it a sequencer fault? Difficult to be certain, but speak with the technical helpline for the sequencer company to see if such a fault has been reported.

Your sequencer syncs up late;

- Have you allowed 10 or 15 seconds run-in at the start of the song for the sequencer to establish the incoming timing?
- If you are using SMPTE time code, have you set the correct Start Time on the sequencer?

Appendix

MIDI program changes

You can remotely change patches on a MIDI instrument by sending it a MIDI program change. Such a message is usually sent when a patch is selected on a synth. Unfortunately, different manufacturers use different numbering systems.

The first column shows the standard MIDI program change numbering, starting from 0. Few instruments actually use this system. The second column shows the system used by some manufacturers and most sequencers. The numbers start from 1, not 0.

The third column shows the method used by synths which have their banks organised in sets of eight. The fourth column is identical except that a letter is used in place of a bank number.

Finally, the fifth column shows the method used by synths which have their banks organised in sets of sixteen.

Table 1 - Program change table

0	1	1-1	A-1	A-1
1	2	1-2	A-2	A-2
2	3	1-3	A-3	A-3
3	4	1-4	A-4	A-4
4	5	1-5	A-5	A-5
5	6	1-6	A-6	A-6
6	7	1-7	A-7	A-7
7	8	1-8	A-8	A-8
8	9	2-1	B-1	A-9
9	10	2-2	B-2	A-10
10	11	2-3	B-3	A-11
11	12	2-4	B-4	A-12
12	13	2-5	B-5	A-13

13	14	2-6	B-6	A-14
14	15	2-7	B-7	A-15
15	16	2-8	B-8	A-16
16	17	3-1	C-1	B-1
17	18	3-2	C-2	B-2
18	19	3-3	C-3	B-3
19	20	3-4	C-4	B-4
20	21	3-5	C-5	B-5
21	22	3-6	C-6	B-6
22	23	3-7	C-7	B-7
23	24	3-8	C-8	B-8
24	25	4-1	D-1	B-9
25	26	4-2	D-2	B-10
26	27	4-3	D-3	B-11
27	28	4-4	D-4	B-12
28	29	4-5	D-5	B-13
29	30	4-6	D-6	B-14
30	31	4-7	D-7	B-15
31	32	4-8	D-8	B-16
32	33	5-1	E-1	C-1
33	34	5-2	E-2	C-2
34	35	5-3	E-3	C-3
35	36	5-4	E-4	C-4
36	37	5-5	E-5	C-5
37	38	5-6	E-6	C-6
38	39	5-7	E-7	C-7
39	40	5-8	E-8	C-8
40	41	6-1	F-1	C-9
41	42	6-2	F-2	C-10
42	43	6-3	F-3	C-11
43	44	6-4	F-4	C-12
44	45	6-5	F-5	C-13
45	46	6-6	F-6	C-14
46	47	6-7	F-7	C-15
47	48	6-8	F-8	C-16
48	49	7-1	G-1	D-1
49	50	7-2	G-2	D-2
50	51	7-3	G-3	D-3
51	52	7-4	G-4	D-4
52	53	7-5	G-5	D-5
53	54	7-6	G-6	D-6
54	55	7-7	G-7	D-7
55	56	7-8	G-8	D-8
56	57	8-1	H-1	D-9
57	58	8-2	H-2	D-10
58	59	8-3	H-3	D-11
59	60	8-4	H-4	D-12
60	61	8-5	H-5	D-13
61	62	8-6	H-6	D-14
62	63	8-7	H-7	D-15
63	64	8-8	H-8	D-16
64	65	9-1	I-1	E-1
65	66	9-2	I-2	E-2
66	67	9-3	I-3	E-3
67	68	9-4	I-4	E-4
68	69	9-5	I-5	E-5
69	70	9-6	I-6	E-6
70	71	9-7	I-7	E-7
71	72	9-8	I-8	E-8

72	73	10-1	J-1	E-9
73	74	10-2	J-2	E-10
74	75	10-3	J-3	E-11
75	76	10-4	J-4	E-12
76	77	10-5	J-5	E-13
77	78	10-6	J-6	E-14
78	79	10-7	J-7	E-15
79	80	10-8	J-8	E-16
80	81	11-1	K-1	F-1
81	82	11-2	K-2	F-2
82	83	11-3	K-3	F-3
83	84	11-4	K-4	F-4
84	85	11-5	K-5	F-5
85	86	11-6	K-6	F-6
86	87	11-7	K-7	F-7
87	88	11-8	K-8	F-8
88	89	12-1	L-1	F-9
89	90	12-2	L-2	F-10
90	91	12-3	L-3	F-11
91	92	12-4	L-4	F-12
92	93	12-5	L-5	F-13
93	94	12-6	L-6	F-14
94	95	12-7	L-7	F-15
95	96	12-8	L-8	F-16
96	97	13-1	M-1	G-1
97	98	13-2	M-2	G-2
98	99	13-3	M-3	G-3
99	100	13-4	M-4	G-4
100	101	13-5	M-5	G-5
101	102	13-6	M-6	G-6
102	103	13-7	M-7	G-7
103	104	13-8	M-8	G-8
104	105	14-1	N-1	G-9
105	106	14-2	N-2	G-10
106	107	14-3	N-3	G-11
107	108	14-4	N-4	G-12
108	109	14-5	N-5	G-13
109	110	14-6	N-6	G-14
110	111	14-7	N-7	G-15
111	112	14-8	N-8	G-16
112	113	15-1	O-1	H-1
113	114	15-2	O-2	H-2
114	115	15-3	O-3	H-3
115	116	15-4	O-4	H-4
116	117	15-5	O-5	H-5
117	118	15-6	O-6	H-6
118	119	15-7	O-7	H-7
119	120	15-8	O-8	H-8
120	121	16-1	P-1	H-9
121	122	16-2	P-2	H-10
122	123	16-3	P-3	H-11
123	124	16-4	P-4	H-12
124	125	16-5	P-5	H-13
125	126	16-6	P-6	H-14
126	127	16-7	P-7	H-15
127	128	16-8	P-8	H-16

MIDI control and mode changes

The first 64 control changes are used for parameters that continuously change such as Volume and Pan. These control changes are divided into two sets; #0 - #31 (Most Significant Byte) are used first and provide for 128 possible positions, or levels, and if this is insufficient #32 - #63 (Least Significant Byte) can be used to provide finer adjustment. Only Bank Select (#0, #32) differs in that #32 is used first.

Control changes #64 - #95 are normally used for 'switch' type functions, although this has been changed in recent years. #96 - #101 are used for increment/decrement and parameter selection while #102 - #119 are currently undefined. The final eight are reserved for mode messages.

Names for some functions simply show the default use - other uses are allowed if the manufacturer makes this clear in the documentation. These include control changes #70 - #79, which can be used for either sound or effects modules, and #91 - #95 which are used for effects depths.

Table 2 - Control change table

Control Change	Name
0	Bank Select
1	Modulation Wheel
2	Breath Controller
3	Undefined
4	Foot Controller
5	Portamento Time
6	Data Entry
7	Main Volume
8	Balance
9	Undefined
10	Pan
11	Expression
12	Effect Control 1
13	Effect Control 2
14 - 15	Undefined
16 - 19	General Purpose 1-4
20 - 31	Undefined
32 - 63	LSB for Control Changes 0 - 31
64	Damper/Sustain Pedal

65	Portamento
66	Sostenuto
67	Soft Pedal
68	Legato Footswitch
69	Hold 2
70	Sound Variation / Exciter
71	Harmonic Content / Compressor
72	Release Time / Distortion
73	Attack Rime / Equaliser
74	Brightness / Expander or Noise Gate
75	Undefined / Reverb
76	Undefined / Delay
77	Undefined / Pitch Transposer
78	Undefined / Flange or Chorus
79	Undefined / Special Effects
80 - 83	General Purpose 5-8
84	Portamento Control
85 - 90	Undefined
91	Effects Depth (Effect 1)
92	Tremolo Depth (Effect 2)
93	Chorus Depth (Effect 3)
94	Celeste Depth (Effect 4)
95	Phaser Depth (Effect 5)
96	Data Increment
97	Data Decrement
98	Non-Registered Parameter Number LSB
99	Non-Registered Parameter Number MSB
100	Registered Parameter Number LSB
101	Registered Parameter Number MSB
102 - 119	Undefined
120	All Sound Off
121	Reset All Controllers
122	Local Control
123	All Notes Off
124	Omni Mode Off
125	Omni Mode On
126	Mono Mode On
127	Poly Mode On

Essential glossary

Rather than take up space with a list of words which you will rarely hear, this glossary simply covers the most common ones,

Aftertouch
Extra pressure brought to bear on the key of a synth after it has been initially played. Most sound modules will recognise this, and will use it to change facets of the sound such as pitch bend or modulation. Channel Pressure uses an average value for all notes being pressed while Key Pressure allows for a different value per key.

Channels
With different synths and sound modules connected to a MIDI system, there has to be a way to individually 'speak' to them. A method similar to television is used; MIDI data is sent on one of 16 possible channels and each synth or sound module is 'tuned in' to recognise information intended for it. However, all MIDI information travels along the same cables.

General MIDI
A consumer-aimed addition to MIDI. Any synth or sound module with the General MIDI logo guarantees to support a minimum MIDI specification and so be compatible with any other General MIDI device.

Local On/Off
The ability to split the sounds in a synth from the keyboard, effectively giving a master keyboard and a sound module. Useful function when working with sequencers.

MIDI

In 1982, various manufacturers decided that there needed to be a standard connection between their different synths. The Musical Instrument Digital Interface was created and consists of two rather distinct parts; the information (notes, pitch bend and so on) produced by MIDI circuits, and the MIDI hardware and ports which transmit and receive such information. The use of MIDI ensures that all MIDI products are compatible with each other to a greater or lesser extent.

MIDI controller

Any MIDI device which is being used to transmit MIDI information is generally called a MIDI controller. Examples such as keyboards and MIDI drum pads are the obvious ones, but don't forget guitar synths and Wind controllers. If a keyboard has sounds on-board it tends to be called a synthesiser; a keyboard with no sounds is termed a Master or Mother keyboard and usually has a superior MIDI spec to a synth.

MIDI control changes

Often called MIDI controllers which can confuse them with the item above. MIDI control changes are MIDI messages that are used to alter the performance aspect of MIDI. For instance, moving the modulation wheel on a synth transmits information for this MIDI control change and generally governs the way in which the Low Frequency Oscillator (LFO) of a synth affects the sound with a resulting degree of 'warbling'. There are a total of 128 MIDI control changes, eight of which are reserved for special MIDI mode messages and some are, as yet, undefined.

MIDI file

A common file format for the saving of songs on a sequencer leading to a high degree of compatibility in the transfer of song data.

MIDI implementation chart

Outlines which of the various MIDI functions are transmitted and recognised by a MIDI device and how they are treated. Included in the back of most manuals.

MIDI ports

MIDI information is received at the MIDI In socket of a device, much like an ear. Any MIDI information created in a device is transmitted from the MIDI Out socket, much like a mouth. Information received at the MIDI In socket is retransmitted from the MIDI Thru socket.

MIDI sync

A general title given to the various MIDI messages that keep two sequencers, or a sequencer and a tape record,er in time with each other. MIDI Start, Stop, Continue and Clock messages carry out the various necessary functions while Song Position Pointer allows a sequencer to find its place in the middle of a song. MIDI time code is an alternative type of MIDI sync.

Multi-timbral

Literally meaning 'many sounds', a multi-timbral synth can be viewed as many independent sound modules in a single box. By setting each module to its own MIDI channel, one multi-timbral synth can have many 'instruments' playing at the same time.

Note numbers

Each note on a keyboard has a different number associated with it, and there are 128 of these in all. The middle C of a standard synth is usually numbered 60; add or subtract one as you go up or down a semitone.

Notes on and off

Hitting a key on a synth generates a MIDI Note On; releasing it produces a Note Off. Each of these includes the MIDI channel, note number and velocity for that note.

Omni on/off

Omni On literally means 'All on' and signifies that a device will recognise MIDI information received on any of the 16 MIDI channels.

Polyphony

A measure of the total number of notes that a synth or sound module can play.

Program changes
A MIDI program change message can remotely select up to 128 patches on a synth, sound module or effects unit.

Quantising
Function used on sequencers to correct the timing of notes and other recorded MIDI events.

Sound module (or expander)
If you remove the keyboard part from a synth and place the sound generating circuitry into a separate box you have a sound module! Commonly called an expander, as it expands the number of sounds that you have access to, many people use a Master controller with several sound modules rather than have lots of synths.

System exclusive
Method used by manufacturers to load and save banks of sounds or individual parameters to and from MIDI devices.

Velocity
A measure of how hard a note has been pressed, for a Note On, or how fast the note has been released, for a Note Off. A Note On can have a velocity between 1 and 127; if the velocity is zero, it acts as a Note Off.

Voices
A synth has a number of sound generators, and this number is generally referred to as the number of voices for that synth. More than one voice may be needed to create a sound; for instance, a blend of two different pad sounds may be used internally to produce a particularly rich and warm timbre. Consequently, a 24 voice synth producing such a pad sound would have a polyphony of just 12 notes.

Index

U. K. M. A.

United Kingdom MIDI Association

26 Brunswick Park Gardens
New Southgate
London
N11 1EJ

Tel: 081 368 2245
Fax: 081 368 7918

UKMA is the official MIDI Association for the UK. Launched in April 1990, **UKMA** is an independent organisation funded by membership and the sales of the various official MIDI documents for which **UKMA** are the European distributors. No sponsorship; any advise we give is of an unbiased nature.

UKMA is essentially an information and problem-solving body which keeps its members completely up-to-date with the latest developments within MIDI. It is able to do this through its membership to the MMA (MIDI Manufacturers Association) in the USA, one of the two worldwide authorities which implement changes to the MIDI Specification. A change may be an additional protocol, such as the new MIDI Machine Control, or simply a more detailed explanation of an existing part of the Specification.

UKMA offers telephone support to Individual members, the like of which would be difficult to find in any industry. Can't decide on your next equipment purchase? Need to know more information on the possibilities for your system? Your sequencer won't sync up with your tape recorder? These answers to these questions and many others are at the end of a telephone help-line.

UKMA also deals with the high-end technical problems through various consultants who are experts in their fields. Members to **UKMA** also include most of the MIDI manufacturers such as Akai, Roland, Yamaha, Technics, Korg, Peavey, Cheetah, SSL, DDA, Soundcraft and Allen & Heath to mention but a few, many of whom support **UKMA** with technical information usually unavailable to the public. By this network of members, practically any MIDI problem can be solved.

Benefits for Individual members include:

* MIDI help-line available from 9 a.m. to 9 p.m. most days of the year. Any messages left on the UKMA answer machine are dealt with as quickly as possible. Paging service available.

* Advice on all aspects of MIDI and related areas including equipment purchases, compatibility between MIDI devices in a system, computer software and synchronising.

* MIDI Implementation Charts and System Exclusive documents available for most MIDI devices at a nominal charge.

* Copy of the bi-monthly "MIDI Monitor", a 32-page A4 magazine dedicated to MIDI and including articles across the span of MIDI knowledge from beginner to technical designer.

* 10% discount off all books in the UKMA booklist, dedicated to MIDI and Digital Audio.

Please telephone or write for a free copy of the magazine and a membership form